Biblical Allego

A KEY TO THE MYSTERIES
OF THE KINGDOM OF GOD

(1918)

"The Bible is difficult to understand when taken literally." This rare book gives you the explanations and insight needed to fully appreciate the vast occult wisdom in the Bible. Contents: "De Symbolo"; Introduction; Evil Destroys Itself; Love, the Fulfilling of the Law; Seven Aspects of Man; The Way; At-One-Ment; "These Signs Shall Follow them that Believe."

Frank L. Riley

ISBN 1-56459-605-2

Kessinger Publishing's Rare Reprints
Thousands of Scarce and Hard-to-Find Books!

We kindly invite you to view our extensive catalog list at:
http://www.kessinger.net

CONTENTS

"THE BIBLE ESSENTIAL TO OUR REPUBLIC

" 'I know not how long a republican government can flourish among a great people who have not the Bible. But this I do know, that the existing government of this country could never have had existence but for the Bible. And, further, I do in my conscience believe, that if at every decade of years a copy of the Bible could be found in every family of the land, its republican institutions would be perpetual.

WILLIAM H. SEWARD.' "

(Bible Society Record, January, 1917.)

Do you possess a Bible?

Do you read it?

And what is more important, do you understand what you read?

That a study of the following pages may enlighten the reader, and thus awaken a real love for the Bible, is the sincere desire of the author.

FRANK L. RILEY, M.D.,
1825 N. Bronson Ave.,
Hollywood, Cal.

Dec. 5, 1917.

"DE SYMBOLO"

"Is symbol the husk, the dry bone,
Of the dead soul of ages agone?

.   .   .   .   .   .

"Or is it the screed on the veil
That shuts us off from the pale,—
Strange hieroglyphic print
That the ages unceasingly mint
On the wide world's brazen walls.

.   .   .   .   .   .

"While the stigmata of our soul
Supply us the inner key
To decipher this mystery
Of Nature's palimpsest,
Through which dimly shines confessed
The giant uncial script
Of the Very God's manuscript?"

—Cloudesley Brereton.

.

INTRODUCTION

The Bible Difficult to Understand When Taken Literally

The Bible is probably the most wonderful book in all the world and the most difficult to understand. Many honest students have become agnostics owing to the seeming contradictions which appear in hundreds of passages throughout the Old and New Testaments. A literal interpretation of this Holy Book would lead us to believe that the world was created 4004 B. C.; *that the sun stood still; †that the whale swallowed Jonah; ‡and that our Lord was crucified in Sodom and Egypt.

Ingersoll and Paine Honest Men

Men like ‖Thomas Paine and §Robert G. Ingersoll have spent the best part of their lives ridiculing the Scriptures. This is pathetic, because these brilliant and honest men were ridiculing, not the truth itself; but a literal, which is a

---

*Joshua, x:13.
†Jonah, 1:17.
‡Revelation, xi:8.
‖Thomas Paine, "the son of a Quaker staymaker of Thetford in Norfolk," was born in 1736. He was "the author of The Rights of Man and The Age of Reason." He "would have had a very different kind of a reputation if he had never written these works. Most of those who know him by name as a ribald scoffer against revealed religion are not aware that he has any other title to fame or infamy. But if he had never meddled with religious controversy, his name would have been remembered in the United States at least as one of the founders of their independence.——Encyclopædia Britannica, Vol. XVIII, p. 136.
§Robert G. Ingersoll, an "American lawyer and lecturer, was born in Dresden, New York, 11th August, 1833. His father was a Congregational minister." During the Civil War he was colonel of a cavalry regiment. "He was appointed attorney-general of Illinois in 1866, and in 1876 his speech in the Republican National Convention, naming James G. Blaine for Presidential nomination, won him a national reputation as a public speaker." His lectures included: The Gods and Other Lectures, Some Mistakes of Moses, The Bible, and Foundations of Faith.—Encyclopædia Britannica, Vol. XXIX, p. 489.
The fact that Paine was the son of a Quaker, and Ingersoll the son of a Congregational minister, is not without significance. Dogma never satisfies man's thirst for truth: in spite of all obstacles he continues his quest.

false, interpretation of the Scriptures. They understood that the Bible was meant to be taken literally:
taking it literally, they found it open to criticism; and
they criticized it. It is not to be wondered at that they
thought and wrote and lectured as they did, for it is
difficult in this prosaic, matter-of-fact age to understand the beautiful allegories contained in the Bible
from Genesis to Revelation. Even the clergymen are
"perplexed."

The Clergy   The following extract from a sermon
Perplexed   preached by Dean Inge at St. Paul's Ca-
thedral in London, England, is interesting and sug-
gestive. It indicates that the more advanced preachers
in the Christian Churches are endeavoring to rectify
past mistakes.

*"The four 'last things,' as they used to be called,
Death, Judgment, Heaven, and Hell, seemed to be de-
liberately avoided in modern preaching. The clergy
felt that those four things were not popular, especially
when they were addressing a congregation of working
men. As soon as they left the subjects of this world
and began to talk about Eternity, the men's attention
obviously flagged and their interest grew cold. * * *

"The main cause of the change was that Heaven
had been too often pictured by Christians in such a
way as to deprive it of its religious and spiritual value.
Many Christians were far too materialistic in their
religion, and they tried to make Heaven a geographical
expression and to put Eternity within the framework
of Time. * * * If we put our beliefs in such a
crude and materialistic form, they were little better

*The Times, London, May 22, 1914.

than a fairy tale. We both impoverished the ideal and added a spurious form which could not be defended in argument. There was not the slightest doubt that educated people did suppose the teaching of the Church to be that Heaven was a literal place where God and the Angels lived, and where good people went when they died or after the Day of Judgment, there to be recompensed for the good they had done and the evil they had suffered. But the average man thought for himself, and wanted to know what evidence there was for the existence of such a place, and he knew enough astronomy to feel the absurdity of placing it either inside or outside the solar system. So many of the clergy were perplexed themselves, and said as little about Heaven as they decently could. The time had gone by when people were best taught by gaudy coloured picture-books. They would rather the clergy said that they did not know than have crude symbols given as literal facts."

Bible Allegories   I use the word **allegory** because much of the Bible is composed of beautiful stories which are pure myths or allegories. St. Paul in his espistle to the Galatians clearly states that the story of Abraham and his two wives is an allegory,

*"For it is written, that Abraham had two sons, the one by a bondmaid, the other by a freewoman.

"But he who was of the bondwoman was born after the flesh; but he of the freewoman was by promise.

"Which things are an allegory."

*Galatians, iv:22-24.

To those who have been accustomed to take the Bible literally, this idea of treating its stories purely as allegories may come as a shock at first; but if they persist in the study of the Scriptures from this standpoint, the whole Book will become illumined, and the perusal of its sacred pages will inspire and delight them. Personally I was deeply grieved when I found that the Bible contradicted itself in so many different passages, but since studying it in this new light, I have learned to love it more and more. It is indeed a Book filled with jewels of wisdom; but, as with all other books, search must be made for them.

St. Paul in his second espistle to Timothy writes:

Rightly Divide Word of Truth *"Study to show thyself approved unto God, a workman that needeth not to be ashamed, right dividing the word of truth."

It is always necessary rightly to divide the word of truth, and it is also important for us to remember that we must be workmen. The old dogmatic and threadbare interpretations of the sacred writings must be cast aside, and one must approach this great task with an open mind, free from all misconceptions and preconceived ideas. The honest student need have no fear if he will but remember that it is impossible to destroy truth, and that it never injures truth to throw light upon it. For truth is like pure gold; and it is only the dross that can be destroyed.

Truth is Supreme In that brilliant speech of Gamaliel, when Peter and the other apostles were ar-

*II Timothy. ii:15.

raigned before him, we have this significant passage:

*"And now I say unto you, Refrain from these men, and let them alone: for if this counsel or this work be of men, it will come to nought:

"But if it be of God, ye cannot overthrow it; lest haply ye be found even to fight against God.

"And to him they agreed."

Surely we all agree that since truth is from God, to fight against truth is to endeavour vainly to overthrow God, which idea is unthinkable. And it is this beautiful truth which we shall endeavor to bring to light.

History and Allegory Interwoven There are of course many historical passages in the Bible, and historical cities and persons are mentioned; but this does not disprove the fact that in a large proportion of instances the spiritual interpretation reveals the true and original meaning. Indeed history and allegory or myth are so beautifully interwoven with one another that it is often difficult to discern where history ends and allegory begins, or vice versa. But it must be borne in mind that the Bible was not written primarily as a history.

The Bible "a Hieroglyph of the Soul" The question then naturally arises in the mind of the student: "Why all these myths?"

It should be remembered that these stories are myths in the true sense of the term, and not in the generally accepted sense as "fables and fabulous doc-

*Acts. v:38-40.

trines respecting the deities of heathen nations." Nothing is further from the truth than that these narratives are fables and doctrines respecting the deities of heathen nations, and yet this definition of myth is the one accepted by the man in the street. The true definition of myth, particularly as it relates to the allegories contained in the Bible, would be something as follows: A story or narrative where signs, symbols, numbers, characters, etc., are employed to express an inner or spiritual experience. The whole Bible in fact is *"a hieroglyph of the soul."

Hieroglyph Defined The word hieroglyph is defined as *"a sacred character or symbol in ancient writings; pictures to express historical facts."

The Bible then is filled with innumerable sacred characters and symbols—pictures which express not only historical facts but spiritual facts or experiences.

Myth Defined Max Heindell defines a myth as †"a casket containing at times the deepest and most precious jewels of spiritual truth, pearls of beauty so rare and ethereal that they cannot stand exposure to the material intellect. In order to shield them and at the same time allow them to work upon humanity for its spiritual upliftment, the Great Teachers who guide our evolution unseen but potent, give these spiritual truths to nascent humanity encased in the picturesque symbolism of myths, so that they might work upon his feelings until such time as his dawning intellect should have become sufficiently evolved and spiritualized so that he may both feel and know.

*The Perfect Way, by Anna Kingsford and Edward Maitland. p. 62.
†Rosicrucian Christianity Series—Parsifal. pp. 3, 4.

"This on the same principle that we give our children moral teachings by means of picture books and fairy tales, reserving the more direct teaching for later years."

Biblical Symbolism Varies in Form
We might liken the Bible to a journey from Egypt to Jerusalem, from sense to soul, from matter to Spirit, or from bondage in this world to spiritual freedom. Again, the symbolism takes another form, for we might think of it as the building of a temple.

*"Know ye not that ye are the temple of God, and that the Spirit of God dwelleth in you?

"If any man defile the temple of God, him shall God destroy; for the temple of God is holy, which temple ye are."

It is absolutely impossible for us to understand spiritual facts and experiences except by the use of allegories and symbols. We all know how nursery rhymes and fairy tales and fables about foxes and rabbits are useful in teaching children lessons in morality, as Max Heindel has reminded us in his definition of a myth. Now, we are all children when the mysteries of the kingdom of God are presented for our understanding; and the beautiful allegories contained in the Bible are as necessary for us as are the fairy tales for the children.

Upon one occasion Jesus said to his disciples:

†"Unto you it is given to know the mystery of the kingdom of God; but unto them that are

*I Corinthians. iii.16. 17.
†St. Mark. iv:11.

The Mysteries of the Kingdom of God without, all these things are done in parables."

Again, St. Paul, the great mystic, wrote:

*"But we speak the wisdom of God in a mystery."

†How that by revelation he made known unto me the mystery; (as I wrote afore in few words,

"Whereby, when ye read, ye may understand my knowledge in the mystery of Christ.)

"Which in other ages was not made known unto the sons of men, as it is now revealed unto his holy apostles and prophets by the Spirit."

The above passages clearly show that the Bible is full of mysteries, and that they must be spiritually discerned and properly interpreted before the deeper wisdom underlying them can be ascertained and applied in our daily lives. The wonderful value of this inner teaching lies in the fact that it can be used even in the smallest detail connected with our lives. In this sense the Bible is really true—indeed, it is truth; and one might even go so far as to say that a myth is truer and more real than history, since the myth actually represents the various states or stages of consciousness through which man is to pass in his journey from earth to heaven, or from the without to the within. These mysteries portray the unfolding or the evolving of the soul, whereas material history is nothing more than the shadow or echo of the inner.

*I Corinthians. ii :7.
†Ephesians. iii :3-5.

The Bible Written by Mystics It has been said that *"the Bible was written by mystics for mystics, and from the mystical standpoint; and it has been interpreted by materialists for materialists, and from the materialistic standpoint."

Misleading Translations This being true, we can see how very easy it would be for translators of the original text to give us many misleading translations, especially if they were not versed in the mysteries.

"With Fear and Trembling," an Instance One instance might be given showing how easy it is to mistranslate a passage. In the King James version we read: †"Work out your own salvation with fear and trembling." But we are informed that the word **with** should be translated **in the midst of**. The reader will readily see how difficult it must be to work out one's salvation full of fear and trembling, whereas by God's help one can overcome evil even though surrounded by fear and trembling. Verse 15 (same chapter) also helps to bear out this idea of being "in the midst of" fear and trembling.

> "That ye may be blameless and harmless, the sons of God, without rebuke, **in the midst of** a crooked and perverse nation, among whom ye shine as lights in the world."

Ferrar Fenton translates Philippians, ii:12, 13, as follows:

"Work out your own salvation **amidst** fear and

*The Bible's Own Account of Itself by Edward Maitland. B. A., p. 3.
†Philippians, ii:12.

terror; for God is energizing in you both to will and to do for the sake of His approbation."

Does God Lead Us into Temptation?   Another perplexing verse is found in St. Matthew, vi:13, which reads as follows:

"And lead us not into temptation, but deliver us from evil."

Many earnest Christians have wondered how it would be possible for God (Good) to lead a man into temptation. Ferrar Fenton's translation of this passage solves the mystery. The verse, he tells us, should read as follows:

"For You would not bring us into temptation, but deliver us from its evil."

Referring to his translation of the Lord's Prayer he writes:

*"The above is the literal translation of the original Greek, retaining the Greek moods and tenses by the clearest English I could. The old versions, having been made from a Latin translation, could not reproduce the actual sense of the Saviour as given by the Evangelists, for Latin has no Aorist of the Imperative Passive Mood used by Matthew or Luke."

Difficulties with the Hebrew Text   When we go back to the Hebrew of the Old Testament complications multiply, and the mystery grows deeper, for †"the Hebrew text * * * may be changed by differently placing the vowels and dividing the words in another way.

"There are two well-recognized methods of reading

*The New Testament in Modern English, by Ferrar Fenton, p. 39.
†The Rosicrucian Cosmo-Conception, by Max Heindel, p. 321.

this sentence. One is: *'in the beginning God created the heavens and the earth'; the other is: 'Out of the ever-existing essence the twofold energy formed the double heaven.'"

The reader will observe that the latter translation of the reading of this passage is much clearer and more to the point than the former.

We have high authority in support of allegorism.

Origen Supports Biblical Allegorism   †"Origen, in his commentary on John, declares that, while every passage of Scripture has a spiritual meaning, many passages have no other meaning, but there is often a spiritual meaning under a literal fiction. And he adds that it can be only a narrow intelligence which does not see that Scripture relates events which could not have occurred as described. * * *

St. Gregory, St. Athanasius, St. Dionysius, the Areopagite, Maimonides, All Take Their Stand for the Allegorical Method   "St. Gregory, in his commentary on the book of Kings, says of the entire letter of Scripture that it is 'not only dead, but deadly.' St. Athanasius warns us that, were we to understand sacred writ according to the letter, we should fall into the most enormous blasphemies, as by ascribing cruelty and falsehood to the Deity—which is precisely what the orthodoxists and Agnostics have done. 'St. Dionysius the Areopagite,' characterizes the literal acceptance of Scripture as childishness; and this, as shown by Mosheim, was the view of all the

---

*Genesis, 1:1.
†The Bible's Own Account of Itself, by Edward Maitland, B. A., pp. 9, 10.

Fathers of the second century. And such was the opinion also of the great Rabbinical commentators from Maimonides downwards. * * * Says Dr. Everard, the learned and pious translator from the Arabic of the Hermetic book, 'The Divine Pymander,' in his 'Gospel Treasury Opened' (A.D. 1659): 'I say, there is not one word [of Scripture] true according to the letter. Yet I say that every word, every syllable, every letter, is true. But they are true as He intended them that spake them; they are true as God meant them, not as men will have them.' "

Allegories Transformed into Histories Gerald Massey, in his most interesting treatise, entitled, **A Book of the Beginnings**, tells us that, *"After the allegories had been transformed into histories, the true interpretation, that is the symbolical reading according to the principles of the secret tradition, was forbidden to be taught in schools. The Pharisees were so fearful of the Apocryphal wisdom being unveiled and the secrets made known that they sought to prevent people from writing. * * *

Philo Treats Pentateuch as Allegorical "Philo, the most learned and devout of Jews, treats the Pentateuch as allegorical and symbolical, which is the nature of the sacred writings. * * * He is recognized by Josephus and Eusebius as one of the most illustrious of his race. He appears to have been an initiate in the mysteries as Paul was, and it is vain to explain that he was given to allegorical interpretation when all early sacred writings are allegorical; nor do we arrive at their facts by getting rid of their symbols."

*A Book of the Beginnings, by Gerald Massey, Vol. II.

The following is also worthy of notice:

Story of Creation not to be Taken Literally says Maimonides *"Maimonides, the most learned of the Rabbis, speaking of the Book of Genesis, says, 'We ought not to take literally that which is written in the story of the Creation, nor entertain the same ideas of it as are common with the vulgar. If it were otherwise, our ancient sages would not have taken so much pains to conceal the sense, and to keep before the eyes of the uninstructed the veil of allegory which conceals the truth it contains.' In the same spirit it was ob-

Jerome's Testimony served by Jerome, that 'the most difficult and obscure of the holy books contain as many secrets as they do words, concealing many things even under each word.'"

The City of Alexandria The history of the Bible is so intertwined with that of the wonderful city Alexandria that a peep at it as it appeared 2,000 years ago during the time of Philo may be of interest.

The Alexandrian Libraries It was a city famous for its culture. The patronage extended by the Ptolemies to learning, encouraged teachers of the varying forms of Greek philosophy to settle there with their followers. Philo tells us that the lecture halls in the museum or college were always crowded although the discourses were given daily. Another attraction was its famous libraries, no mean attraction when one considers the costliness and the difficulties of obtaining books in those days. They were founded by Ptolemy Soter, and were the largest and most cel-

*The Perfect Way, by Anna Kingsford. M. D., and Edward Maitland. B. A., p. 149.

ebrated of ancient times. After Ptolemy Soter had conquered Egypt he turned his attention to the formation of the libraries, and under his direction works of art as well as books were collected by experts.

Ptolemy Philadelphus (285-247 B. C.) and Ptolemy Euergetes (247-222 B. C.) carried on the work of increasing the libraries founded by their predecessor.

Philadelphus was responsible for the proper organization of the libraries. There were two; one was established in the Serapeum in the Egyptian quarter of the town, and the other in a building in the Bruchium, the royal or Greek quarter. In the Bruchium there were about 490,000 volumes or rolls, while in the Serapeum there were 42,800 rolls. According to Aulus Gellius there were 700,000 rolls: according to Seneca there were 400,000. But authorities differ as to the number of volumes contained in these two libraries.

An ancient roll was much smaller, we are told, than a modern book, and this fact must be borne in mind when comparing this celebrated collection of books with famous modern libraries.

Enriching the *"Ptolemy Philadelphus sent into every **Collections** part of Greece and Asia to secure the most valuable works, and no exertions or expense were spared in enriching the collections."

The fact that these libraries contained books from every part of Greece and Asia, and that the learned men of Alexandria thus had at their command the wisdom of the ancient world is significant, especially when one remembers that the Septuagint was in the pro-

*Encyclopædia Britannica, Vol. XIV, p. 510.

cess of formation at this time, and that the Alexandrian Jews, or at least Jews in touch with Alexandrian culture, were probably responsible for the Greek translation of the Hebrew Scriptures.

During the reign of Philadelphus, his celebrated librarian Callimachus purchased Aristotle's library, and Jewish and Egyptian books were also added to the libraries.

*"Euergetes * * * largely increased the library by seizing on the original editions of the dramatists laid up in the Athenian archives," and †"is said to have caused all books brought into Egypt by foreigners to be seized for the benefit of the library, while the owners had to be content with receiving copies of them in exchange."

The Alexandrian Schools Hellenic culture was at this time developed under new conditions. There were two distinct Alexandrian schools, the school of poetry and science, and the school of philosophy.

The Destruction of the Larger Library Cæsar burnt the fleet in the Alexandrian harbour, and ‡"the flames accidentally extended to the larger library of the Bruchium, and it was destroyed."

Anthony presented to Cleopatra the Pergamus library in his endeavor to repair the loss.

In 273 A. D., Aurelian destroyed the Bruchium quarter of Alexandria, and it may be that one of the libraries was also destroyed, for from that time the

*Encyclopædia Britannica. Vol. I. p. 498.
†Ibid. Vol. XIV. p. 510.
‡Ibid. Vol. XIV. p. 511.

Serapeum became the more important of the two libraries.

*"In 389 or 391 an edict of Theodosius ordered the destruction of the Serapeum, and its books were pillaged by the Christians. When we take into account the disordered condition of the times, and the neglect into which literature and science had fallen, there can be little difficulty in believing that there were but few books left to be destroyed by the soldiers of 'Amr."

The Final Destruction of the Libraries The story of the final destruction of the libraries, however, is interesting whether it be true or not.

In the year A. D. 641, the Arabians under 'Amr had succeeded in taking Alexandria after a fourteen months' Siege. 'Amr at the request of John the Grammarian wrote to the caliph Omar for his instructions respecting the library.

Omar replied as follows:

†"As to the books you have mentioned, if they contain what is agreeable with the book of God, in the book of God is sufficient without them; and if they contain what is contrary to the book of God, there is no need of them; so give orders for their destruction." The priceless books were then burned in the fires that heated the public baths. It is stated by one historian that six months elapsed before they were all consumed.

Thus we see what religious fanaticism will cause men to do.

"The history of Alexandrine Platonism in the Chris-

*Encyclopædia Britannica, Vol. XIV, p. 511.
†Ibid, Vol. VII, p. 749.

Alexandrine Platonism tian Church" is worthy of careful study by all students of primitive Christianity. The writings of Philo and the Gnostics, and later those of Clement and Origen, made a profound impression on the early Christians, and resulted in a *"crisis in the history of the Church. * * *

"It was not without reason that the first systematic attempt to harmonize the tradition of faith with the free conclusions of human intellect was made neither at Rome nor at Athens, but in Egypt. * * * Alexandria still possessed its three great royal foundations, the Museum, the Serapeum, and the Sebastion; its three libraries, its clerical heads, its well-endowed staff of professors and sinecure fellows. Nor did these misuse their advantages. Though the hope of imperial favour drew the more ambitious teachers of philosophy and rhetoric irresistibly towards Rome, letters were still cultivated, and the exact sciences flourished as nowhere else by the banks of the Nile."

†"Greek philosophy began to look towards Oriental mysticism or positive revelation to satisfy its yearnings. The religious spirit of the East, on its side, could not resist the fascination of Greek intellect and learning."

Thus the happy blending of East and West in Egypt produced what is now known as ‡"the Jewish Alexandrian and Neo-Platonic schools."

Philo was the most noted exponent of the former school.

‖"The Jews of Egypt, if we may credit Philo,

*The Christian Platonists of Alexandria, by Charles Bigg D.D., pp. 25, 26.
†Philo Judaeus, by James Drummond, LL.D., pp. 6, 7.
‡Ibid. p. 7.
‖The Christian Platonists of Alexandria, by Charles Bigg D.D., p. 26.

The Jews of Egypt numbered not less than a million souls. In no city of the Empire were they so wealthy or so powerful as at Alexandria."

It must be remembered that the Jews had been very greatly influenced by the Greeks.

*"They were deeply impressed by that irresistible force which was blending all races and nations into one great cosmopolitan unity, and so the Jews too on their dispersion became in speech and nationality Greeks, or rather 'Hellenists.' Now the distinguishing character of Hellenism is not the absolute disappearance of Oriental civilizations before that of Greece, but the combination of the two with the preponderance of the Greek element. So it was with the Jews, but in their case the old relation had much more persistence than in other Hellenistic circles. * * * This Hellenistico-Judaic phase of culture is sometimes called 'Alexandrian,' and the expression is justifiable if it only means that in Alexandria it attained its highest development and flourished most. For here the Jews began to busy themselves with Greek literature even under their clement rulers, the first Ptolemies, and here the law and other Scriptures were first translated into Greek; here the process of fusion began earliest and proceeded with greatest rapidity; here, therefore, also the Jews first engaged in a scientific study of Greek philosophy and transplanted that philosophy to the soil of Judaism."

The Origin and Development of Allegorism It is highly important that at this juncture we should make a careful inquiry into the origin and development of allegorism or the allegorical method.

*Encyclopaedia Britannica, Vol. XVIII, p. 760.

The Encyclopædia Britannica in an article on Philo tells us that

"**The allegorical method had been practiced before Philo's date in the rabbinical schools of Palestine,** and he himself expressly refers to its use by his predecessors, nor does he feel that any further justification is requisite."

This method was not practiced in Palestine alone.

The ancient Hindu Scriptures, including the Vedas, the Upanishads and the Bhagavad-Gitâ can be no more understood when taken literally than can our Bible; and this statement also applies to the Buddhist Scriptures. The writings of Lao-tze and Kwang-tze are full of allegories; and the Zend-Avesta and the Book of the Dead are an enigma without the application of the allegorical method of interpretation.

In every race, even among aboriginal tribes, myths, allegories and symbols are to be found. A whole volume would be required to discuss this subject in detail.

A Settled Code of Laws   The more one studies this fascinating problem the more is one convinced that there is a "settled code of laws," which when employed will interpret or unlock nearly all the sacred writings of the world.

The following quotation from **Philo Judaeus** throws some light upon the subject.

*"Philo tells us that 'almost everything, or most things in the legislation [that is, I presume, in the Pentateuch] are related allegorically.'"

It is supposed that the allegorical interpretation or explanation of Scripture *"had long been familiar

*Philo Judaeus, by James Drummond LL.D., Vol. I. p. 20.

to the Egyptian Jews. It seems, accordingly in Philo's time to have been characteristic of a school of expositors, to have attained to the regularity of a system, as we may judge from the retention of the same symbolical meaning for the same person or event, and to have been governed by a settled code of laws or canons."

It is not to be wondered at that we now find a difficulty in unlocking the Scriptures. The burning of the Alexandrian libraries, the destruction of thousands of precious documents by religious fanatics during the dark ages, and the deliberate attempt of teachers for hundreds of years to conceal the Truth have left this age in darkness and doubt—but not in despair. Truth cannot always be hidden, and can never be destroyed. Like gold, it has been purified by the very fire through which it has passed, and has been made more glorious and beautiful. It fairly scintillates as the accretion of the ages is removed.

Allegorism the Key to the Riddles The "key," always known to a few of the faithful, is now coming more and more into general use; and that "key" is allegorism.

The human race grows hungry for the mysteries of the kingdom of God; and praise be to God, He will not leave us comfortless, for He is divine Love: He is only too willing to feed us. He is the Light of the world, and the instant we open the window of our consciousness it will be flooded with the rays which are for ever radiating from the great Universal Soul.

Every word of the following passage by Dr. Bigg

regarding "the Key to the riddles of the Old Testament" should be thoroughly digested:

*"The rest of the Old Testament, though in one sense transient, has yet an eternal significance as 'the shadow of good things to come,' as revealing Christ throughout, though but in riddles and symbols. * * *

"The method by which this inner harmony is discoverable, the key to the riddles of the Old Testament, is Allegorism. * * * By the Christian it was adapted to fresh purposes—the explanation of Prophecy and of the New Testament itself. It was in universal use, and was regarded by all as one of the articles of the Ecclesiastical Canon or Tradition. * * * The Alexandrines differed from their contemporaries in three important points. They regarded **Allegorism Handed Down Through a Succession of Teachers** Allegorism as having been handed down from Christ and a few chosen Apostles, through a succession, not of Bishops, but of Teachers. They employed it boldly, as Philo had done before them, for the reconciliation of Greek culture with the Hebrew Scriptures. And lastly they applied it to the New Testament, not merely for the purpose of fanciful edification, but with the serious object of correcting the literal, mechanical, hierarchical tendencies of the day. This is in truth the noblest side of Allegorism, for here it deals with cases, where the antithesis of letter and spirit is most real and vital."

If it be true that Allegorism was handed down by Christ through a succession of Teachers, then it behooves us to study the Bible carefully and prayerfully in that light.

*The Christian Platonists of Alexandria, by Charles Bigg, D.D., pp. 85-87.

The Allegorical Method is no Fantastic Invention

Many at the present time look upon the spiritual or allegorical interpretation of Scripture as the fantastic invention of a few dreamers, and therefore as unworthy of serious consideration. James Drummond warns us against this hasty conclusion in the following words:

*"We should wholly misapprehend the nature of this system, if we supposed that it consisted either in a mere whimsical search for hidden meanings, or in an intentional falsification of the plain sense of Scripture in order to commend it to philosophical minds."

A War of Words

The following passage from **Philo Judaeus** is cited to show how universal the allegorical method had become. We would not endorse all the teachings of the different schools of philosophy mentioned. To their credit, however, we would say that much which they had written has been misunderstood by the average mind. Many of the differences that separate religion from religion and sect from sect are more seeming than real. Often the controversies between their members are nothing more than a war of words. But the time for unity has arrived—the time to seek, not for differences but for points of agreement in the different religions and philosophies. Unity and love are the words of the hour; and blessed is he who works to this end.

The Evolution of Allegorism

†"With the progress of thought it became impossible for cultured men to accept the ancient mythology in its literal meaning,

*Philo Judaeus, by James Drummond LL.D., Vol. I. p. 18.
†Ibid. Vol. I. p. 121.

and yet, hallowed as it was by long tradition, by the
splendour of the poetry in which it was enshrined, and
by popular veneration, it presented claims to respect
which it was difficult to resist. * * * (The allegorical) method made its appearance among the older
philosophers, for instance, in Democritis, and in Me-
trodorus of Lampsacus, and other followers of Anaxa-
goras, * * * gained increasing favour in the
period of the Sophists, was occasionally used by Aristotle, and received a wider extension from the Cynics.
It was, however, reserved for the Stoics to bring it to
its full development. * * * Happily, two works
proceeding from this school have been preserved, *
* * one by Heraclitus, on 'Homeric Allegories,' the
other by Cornutus, on 'The Nature of the Gods.' "

Dähne finds in a certain passage of the Septuagint
the Pythagorean doctrine of numbers.

The following illuminating passages concerning
the illustrious Origen and his teachings are of great
interest. Dr. Briggs writes:

Origen's   *"Origen, like Clement, held firmly to the
Testimony   unity and inspiration of all Scripture, and
therefore, like Clement, he was driven to find the
answer to this question in Allegorism. There is however considerable difference in detail between the two
teachers.

"Clement is content to accept Allegorism as a fact,
as a part of Tradition. It was sanctioned by the practice of Philo and Barnabas, and appeared to derive
authority from certain passages of Scripture. This
is not enough for Origen, whose reason works always

*The Christian Platonists of Alexandria, by Charles Bigg D.D., pp. 172-179.

with a broad poetic sweep, and never rests till it has
brought the particular affirmation under the scope of
some all-embracing law. To him Allegorism is only
one manifestation of the sacramental mystery of Na-
The law of   ture. There are two heavens, two earths
Corre-   —the visible is but the blurred copy of
spondence   the invisible. The divine wisdom and
goodness, which are the cause of both, are in this
world of ours distorted by refraction arising from the
density of the medium. Yet they may be discerned
by those who have eyes to see. Allegorism, Teleolgy,
the argument from Analogy are all different aspects of
one great truth. * * * For God has so ordered His
creation, has so linked the lower to the higher by
subtle signatures and affinities, that the world we see
is, as it were, a great staircase, by which the mind of
man must climb upwards to Spiritual intelligence.

"From this Law of Correspondence springs inci-
dentally the profound observation that suggested the
Analogy. 'He, who believes the Scripture to have
proceeded from Him who is the Author of Nature, may
well expect to find the same sort of difficulties in it as
are found in the constitution of Nature.' * * * *

Origen "held that innumerable passages in both
Testaments have no sense at all except as allegories.
* * * Many passages of Scripture, he says, are
excluded from belief by physical impossibility. Such
are those which speak of morning and evening before
the creation of the Sun, the story of the Fall, and the
carrying up of our Lord into an exceeding high mountain by Satan in the Temptation."

If many passages are not literally true, then why, urged his critics, are they found in the Bible?

"To this he replied that, though in one sense untrue, they are in another the highest, the only valuable truth. * * * They are the rough outer husk, which repels the ignorant and unfit reader, but stimulates the true child of God to increased exertion. The letter is the external garb, often sordid and torn; but 'the king's daughter is all glorious within.' It is as if the sunlight streamed in through the crannies of a ruinous wall; the wall is ruinous in order that the sunlight may stream in."

*"All Scripture becomes transparent beneath his touch; the 'crannies in the wall' multiply and widen, till the wall itself disappears."

Philo's Method of Interpretation The following extracts will give the reader a slight idea of Philo's method of interpreting the Scriptures. _

"Philo says:

†" 'The perceptive faculty may be regarded in two aspects, the habitual, that is the permanent capacity which we possess whether we exercise it or not, and the operative. Of these, the former is one of the intrinsic powers of the mind, and was generated at the same time. But not so the latter; it sprang subsequently into being, as a helper and ally of the mind.

The Creation of Eve This has been taught by Moses through the mythical account of the creation of Eve—a narrative which must be taken allegorically, for no one could believe that a woman was really made

---

*The Christian Platonists of Alexandria, by Charles Bigg, D.D., p. 184.
†Philo Judaeus, by James Drummond, LL.D., Vol. I, pp. 344,5.

out of a man's rib. Clearly rib stands here for power, as when we say that man has ribs instead of strength, or that an athlete is thick-ribbed. Adam, then, must represent the mind, Eve perception already acting through the senses, and the rib the permanent faculty still dormant in the mind. Now, in order that Eve should be created, it was necessary that Adam should fall asleep; for in reality, when the mind is asleep, perception arises; and when it awakes again, perception is extinguished. This is proved by experience. Whenever we desire to follow a train of exact thought, we retreat to a solitary place, close our eyes and ears, and bid farewell to the senses. Thus, when the mind is wide awake, perception perishes. * * * But even operative perception is, like woman, susceptible rather than active. * * * Consistently with this explanation Adam said, when Eve was brought to him, "This now a bone from my bones, and flesh from my flesh." The word "this" distinguishes the operative from the habitual perception, which is not taken out of the mind, but grows up with it. "Bone" symbolizes power; and "flesh from my flesh" signifies that perception is never independent of the mind, for the latter is its fountain, and the foundation on which it rests.' "

Did God Swear?   Philo's explanation of "God swears" is equally instructive.

*"When it is said that God swears (as in Ex. xiii:11) we have to consider whether this is declared as in reality attaching to him, since it has seemed to very many to be inappropriate. For an oath suggests a testimony about something that is disputable, but to

*Philo Judaeus, by James Drummond, LL.D., Vol. II, pp. 12-14.

God nothing is obscure or disputable, and he requires no witness. * * * Why, then, did the Hierophant [Moses] think proper to introduce him as swearing? In order that he might at the same time confute and console our weakness. * * * (We are) unable to think of anything apart from ourselves, or to escape from our own destinies, sunk in the mortal like snails, or wrapt in a ball, like hedgehogs, round ourselves, we form our thoughts both about the Blessed and Incorruptible and about ourselves. * * * Therefore **No Anthropo-** we attribute to him hands, feet, ingress, **morphic God** egress, enmities, alienations, wrath—parts and passions inappropriate to the Cause. Among these is included the oath, an aid to our weakness. * * * We must remove, then, everything begotten, mortal, mutable, profane, from our thought of God, the unbegotten, and incorruptible, and unchangeable, and holy, and only blessed."

Philo also asserts that mortals "have thoughts about the Cause of all which are similar to those that they entertain about themselves. * * * He (God) required no eyes; for eyes have no perception without sensible light, and sensible light is created; but God saw before creation, using himself as light. * * *"

The Love and In the following excerpt Philo explains **Fear of God** why some men love God, while others fear Him.

"For all the commandments tend towards either the love or the fear of the Self-existent. To those who do not in thought ascribe to the self-existent Being either part or passion of man, but, in a manner worthy of God, honour it on account of itself alone, love is most appropriate; but to all others fear."

In the third chapter of Genesis, verses 8 and 9 we read:

> "And they heard the voice of the Lord God walking in the garden in the cool of the day: and Adam and his wife hid themselves from the presence of the Lord God amongst the trees of the garden.   ·
>
> "And the Lord God called unto Adam, and said unto him, Where art thou?"

Philo evidently had the above or some similar Bible passage in mind when he wrote:

The Cause not *"It would be impious and silly,   *   *   *
Contained in to imagine that God really planted a par-
the Effect adise, as though he wanted luxurious resting-places, for not even the entire cosmos would be a worthy dwelling for God, the universal Ruler; for he is his own place, and we cannot suppose that the cause is contianed in the effect."

The   Alexandria and the Alexandrians are of
Septuagint special interest to us because, as previously remarked, the city is connected with the history of the Septuagint.

The Septuagint is the Alexandrian, and therefore a Greek, version of the Old Testament.

The study of this translation gives us food for reflection, and raises in our minds the question as to how far the translators were influenced by the various religions and philosophies in existence at that time.

*Philo Judaeus, by James Drummond. LL.D., Vol. II, p. 42.

The question also as to when and how the Septuagint came into being is not definitely settled by the scholars: there are differences of opinion on the subject.

The Letter of Aristeas   There is a legend based upon a letter called the Letter of Aristeas, which is in substance as follows:

*"Demetrius Phalereus, keeper of the Alexandrian library, proposed to King Ptolemy II. Philadelphus to have a Greek translation of the Jewish law made for the library. The king consented and sent an embassy, of which the author of the letter was a member, to the high priest Eleazar at Jerusalem asking him to send six ancient, worthy, and learned men from each of the twelve tribes to translate the law for him at Alexandria. Eleazar readily consented and sent seventy-two men with a precious roll of the law. They were most honourably received at the court of Alexandria and conducted to the Island (Pharus), that they might work undisturbed and isolated. When they had come to an agreement upon a section Demetrius wrote down their version; the whole translation was finished in seventy-two days. The Jewish community of Alexandria was allowed to have a copy, and accepted the version officially,—indeed a curse was laid upon the introduction of any changes in it."

Scholars of the present day look upon this letter as spurious.

†"The forgery, however, is a very early one." * * * and "it is probable that the Jewish philosopher Aristobulus, who lived under Ptolemy Philometer (180-

145), derived his account of the origin of the LXX from this **Letter**, with which it corresponds."

The Origin of the Septuagint The Septuagint probably came into being at different periods. In **How we got our Bible** we read: "It was made at different times, beginning somewhere about 280 B. C., and was the version commonly used by the Evangelists and Apostles."

*"It has always been taken as a fact that the version originated at Alexandria, that the law was translated first, and that this took place in the time of Ptolemy II."

The Septuagint was probably written to meet the needs of the Jews, and was translated by Jews who were †"guided by the living tradition which had its focus in the synagogal lessons."

The Importance of the Septuagint But why is the Septuagint so important? Because ‡"it is probably the oldest translation of considerable extent that ever was written, and at any rate it is the starting-point for the history of Jewish interpretation and the Jewish view of Scripture. * * * It is also the key to the New Testament and all the literature connected with it."

The fact that the evangelists and the apostles used the Septuagint accounts for the difference between passages in the New Testament quoted from the Old, and those passages themselves in the Old Testament, for our authorized version of the Old Testament is

*Encyclopædia Britannica. Vol. XXI. p. 667.
†Ibid. p. 663.
‡Ibid. p. 669.

translated from the Hebrew. The New Testament is of course translated from Greek—the language in which it was originally written.

Translators Were Alexandrian Jews The reader should keep in mind that the Septuagint was translated by Alexandrian Jews.

To us this is most important for Philo tells us that the Jews of Alexandria during his lifetime, and in fact for many generations prior to that period, believed in the allegorical interpretation of Scripture.

These early translators were in a far better position to be judges of this matter than we are at the present day. They were earnest students and honest investigators and were able to ascertain facts from documents which have long since been destroyed, and from traditions and mysteries long forgotten except by the very few.

*"The translators," Drummond tells us, "must at least have had some general acquaintance with the popular forms of Greek speculation, and certain tendencies of mind are betrayed by their modifications of the Hebrew text. * * *

"That God was invisible and incapable of such a feeling as repentance was a universal tenet of Greek philosophy; and without any immediate dependence on the doctrine of the philosophers the translators may well have derived this belief from the general influences of the culture amid which they lived. Zeller adds a parenthetical doubt whether we need have recourse to foreign influence at all. This doubt is surely reasonable. Faith in the spirituality and perfection of God

*Philo Judaeus, by James Drummond LL D., Vol. I, pp. 157-159.

is the natural outgrowth of Hebrew religion, and it is well known that the Targums, which represent the more purely Jewish tradition, contain softenings of anthropomorphic expressions precisely similar in character to those which occur in the LXX."

The Golden Thread of Truth How far the Jews influenced the Greeks and were influenced by them, it is difficult to decide. It is perhaps a matter of small importance. Truth is universal and no one religion or philosophy contains all the truth. Numbers of ideas are common to them all. There is but one God, and therefore but one golden thread of Truth. The various religions and philosophies are beads. The wise man is he who strings the beads on the golden thread, thus making one grand unity.

Peace and Brotherhood The more earnestly we look to see where we agree in religious matters the more quickly will peace and brotherhood reign on earth.

Dr. Bigg tells us that there was a movement on foot *"to appropriate Greek wisdom, and to justify the appropriation; to reconcile Judaism with the culture of the Western world. Even before the completion of the Septuagint this tendency was at work. Platonism is discoverable in the Pentateuch."

The Unity of the Scriptures †"The second great question arising out of the completion of the Canon was that of the Unity of Scripture. This the Catholic strenuously asserted."

The above is also an important assertion since the

---

*The Christian Platonists of Alexandria, by Charles Bigg, D.D., p. 29.
†Ibid. p. 82.

"Unity of Scripture" helps to prove the allegorical method to be the right method.

What is meant by the Unity of Scripture?

We understand by this term that the Bible is a perfect whole despite the fact that it was written at different periods by different men.

We cannot divorce the Old Testament from the New; the latter is the fulfillment or consummation of the former. The Old Testament is a preparation for the birth of the Christ; here we have a word picture of the "old man" together with his victories and defeats; we see man gradually developing until the time arrives, spiritually speaking, for the new birth—the birth of the Christ.

The reader, when confused, should go back to the definition of the Bible—"a hieroglyph of the soul."

The Bible tells us the truth about man. There is but one Truth, hence the Unity of Scripture.

There is but one God, one Truth, one universal brotherhood of man, and one inspired Word of God. And it should be remembered that the one Truth is contained in many Sacred Books. What a great day it will be when mankind awakens to this stupendous fact!

Search for the Golden Thread "Seek and ye shall find," we read in Scripture. And when we search for this golden thread of Scriptural unity, we are sure to find it. The search is sweet and inspiring.

Whether the Septuagint *"grew up gradually" or

---

*"The story of Aristeas has long been given up. Even that of Aristobulus appears to be now generally rejected. According to the later the tradition of the Law was made by the order and at the expense of Ptolemy Philadelphus, whose instigator and agent was Demetrius Phalerus; * * * But, as Scaliger first pointed out, Hermip-

was made by seventy wise men under the immediate
patronage of Ptolemy Philadelphus is not known."

The former view is probably the correct one; and if
so we can see how easy it would be for current ideas to
creep into the context during the translation.

**Bible
Contains
Wisdom
of the Ages**

It is our opinion that the Bible contains
the quintessence of all the wisdom of the
ages. It was written by wise men, and
without wisdom it cannot be interpreted.

After all, we are not much concerned with when and
where the Bible was written and translated. The questions we should ask ourselves are:

Do we study the Bible?

Do we understand what we read?

And above all do we love and practice the Truth
contained in the Bible?

**Short
Account
of Philo,
Origen,
St. Athanasius
and others**

We have quoted far-reaching statements
by Philo, Origen, St. Athanasius, and
others. Any man can make bold asser-
tions: it is well, therefore, to ascertain
both the standing and qualifications of
the men making the statements.

*For the benefit of those readers who have not

---

pus, a writer of very good note, relates that Demetrius Phalereus was banished by Philadelphus, whose succession to the throne he had endeavoured to prevent. This error dis-
credits the whole statement by Aristobulus, and it is accordingly more than doubtful
whether the translation of the Pentateuch was in any way encouraged by Philadelphus.
* * * By some the translation is supposed to have grown up gradually out of a cus-
tom introduced by Ezra. By the side of the reader of the Law stood an interpreter (Me-
turgeman) who translated the lessons from Hebrew into the vernacular tongue. * * *
It is certain that the Septuagint Version was made at different times by different
hands. The Pentateuch, the oldest portion, dates from the first half of the third century B.C."

(The Christian Platonists of Alexandria, by Charles Bigg, D.D., p. 22.)

*From the pages of the Encyclopædia Britannica we obtain an unbiased and un-
sectarian account of the celebrated scholars to whom we have referred. Sectarianism
is liable to make men blind to the truth; and sectarian writers are rarely able to offer
an unbiased account of those who are considered by them to be unorthodox. We feel
therefore that no better authority can be cited: hence the numerous quotations.

made a study of the biographies of the Church Fathers we append a short account of these men, where they lived, what they taught, and the opinion of their fellows with regard to them.

The marvelous unanimity of opinion of these writers, that the Scriptures must, from Genesis to Revelation be interpreted allegorically, should strike the most casual and superficial reader as significant.

It will be observed that they all lived at some period of their lives in Egypt, and that all but one resided from time to time in Alexandria.

PHILO

Philo Judaeus was born about 15 B. C.

He was of good birth and his family was well known in Alexandria, where he is supposed to have spent the whole of his life.

He is without doubt the most distinguished advocate of Hellentistic Judaism, and his various works are considered by scholars to give us the most lucid explanation as to what this phase of Judaism really was.

The following extract gives us Philo's views with regard to asceticism, temperance and hypocrisy. From this citation we gather that he was a practical man as well as a philosopher.

Philo no Ascetic *"Philo was not an ascetic. He indeed believed that the beatific vision of God could be reached only by the control of the senses and passions; but this control was not to be attained by artificial methods. He had learned from his allegory

---

*Philo Judaeus, by James Drummond. LL. D., Vol. I. pp. 24-5.

that the serpent pleasure bites in the wilderness; and he found in his own experience that often when he had left his friends and his home, and gone into the desert, that he might contemplate some of the things worth beholding, he gained no benefit, but his mind was dissipated, or bitten by passion; but sometimes in the midst of a crowd he secluded his soul, and thus was taught that 'it is not the differences of places that work the good or ill, but God, who moves and guides the chariot of the soul wherever he prefers.' **Accordingly he (Philo) lived in the world, while he tried to keep himself from its evil.** * * * Instead of fleeing from the banquet-table,—such was Philo's idea—exhibit there the virtue of temperance. Those who, with squalid and melancholy exterior, say that they despise glory and pleasure are only hypocrites."

A Practical Philo was evidently a mystic, and the
Mystic fact that he was able to seclude his soul in the midst of a crowd reminds one of the statement of Jesus: "The kingdom of God is within you;" also that man must learn to enter his closet, and when the door is shut, pray to the Father in secret.

We need more men to-day who can live in the world and yet keep themselves from its evil.

Again we read that Philo *"did not intend to step into the arena as the champion of a new philosophy, but rather to present an apologia for the teaching of Moses by showing that, even where it appeared questionable or trifling, it was full of the highest philosophical truth. His philosophy, therefore, only came in by the way, and is guided by the requirements of

---

*Philo Judaeus, by James Drummond, LL.D., Vol. I, pp. 1, 2.

Philo Occupies Unique Historical Position

his Biblical interpretation. Precisely for this reason he occupies a unique historical position, and has attained an eminence which, perhaps, on purely Hellenic ground he could hardly have reached. He became a model for the early Christian theologians, and especially for those of Alexandria. His general method of exegesis, many of its details, the determining principles of his religious philosophy, passed into the Christian Church."

Date of Philo's Works

Most of Philo's works were probably written before 38 A.D. It is possible that his writings *"may have been known to some of the writers of the New Testament, and there are occasionally startling coincidences of thought and expression, yet there is nothing to prove conscious borrowing, and it is probable that the resemblances are due to the general condition of religious culture among the Jews."

Doctrine of the Logos

The doctrine of the Logos was probably the chief factor of Philo's philosophy. This doctrine was taught before his time but he elaborated it.

Philo often quotes the Greek poets and tragedians, and it is quite evident that he had studied the works of Plato, Heraclitus, Pythagoras and the Stoics. He had so carefully studied and identified himself with the Greek philosophy that one might reasonably say that he was himself a Greek philosopher. He combined the various philosophies in such a wonderful way, and

*Philo Judaeus, by James Drummond, LL.D., Vol. I, p. 12.

brought out the unity underlying them all so clearly, that one might say that he actually had a philosophy of his own. Although Philo had been greatly influenced by Greek philosophy, nevertheless, he found in the Pentateuch everything that was taught by the Greeks.

Philo a Monotheist   Philo was a monotheist: he believed in *"the absolute majesty and sovereignty of God above the world," and "the principle that He is to be worshipped without images. * * * The specifically Jewish (i.e., particularistic) conception of the election of Israel, the obligation of the Mosaic law, the future glory of the chosen nation, have almost disappeared; he is really a cosmopolitan and praises the Mosaic law just because he deems it cosmopolitan."

Paved the Way for Advent of Christianity   If "the determining principles of his religious philosophy passed into the Christian Church," and if he, the most distinguished of the Hellenistic Jews, through his teaching and writings paved the way for the advent of Christianity, then it behooves every earnest student to study carefully his principal works. Such a noble soul is worthy of our profound respect and admiration.

ST. DIONYSIUS THE AREOPAGITE

†"Dionysius, the Areopagite, according to Sudias, was an Athenian by birth, and eminent for his literary attainments. He studied first at Athens, and afterwards at Heliopolis in Egypt. * * * (He) re-

*Encyclopædia Britannica, Vol. XVIII. p. 761.
†Ibid. Vol. VII. p. 248.

turned to Athens, he was admitted into the Areopagus, and, having embraced Christianity about 50 A.D., was constituted Bishop of Athens by the Apostle Paul (Acts xvii, 34.) Aristides, an Athenian philosopher, asserts he suffered martyrdom—a fact generally admitted by historians."

CLEMENT OF ALEXANDRIA

Little is known of the history of Titus Flavius Clemens "the Alexandrian." He lived probably during the reign of the Emperor Severus, forsook heathenism for Christianity, and became a presbyter in the church of Alexandria. He numbered Origen among his pupils.

*"Clement occupies a profoundly interesting position in the history of Christianity. He is the first to bring all the culture of the Greeks and all the speculations of the Christian heretics to bear on the exposition of Christian truth. He does not attain to a systematic exhibition of Christian doctrine, but he paves the way for it, and lays the first stones of the foundation."

He believed in the unity and in the inspiration of the Scriptures, and Dr. Bigg is in order when he tells us that Clement regarded Allegorism as an inherited tradition.

ORIGEN

Origen was known as the man with an "eagle eye." He certainly was able to get at the core of things, and his spiritual perception was remarkable.

He was born in the year 185 A. D.

*Encyclopædia Britannica, Vol. V. p. 820.

Origen Father of the Church's Science *"Of all the theologians of the ancient church, with the possible exception of Augustine, Origen is the most distinguished and the most influential. He is the father of the Church's science; he is the founder of a theology which was brought to perfection in the 4th and 5th centuries, and which still retained the stamp of his genius when in the 6th century it disowned its author. It was Origen who created the dogmatic of the church and laid the foundations of the scientific criticism of the Old and New Testaments."

In looking back through the pages of history we frequently observe that the founder of some great movement, school, sect or philosophy is repudiated for a time by the very persons who have profited most by his teachings.

Truth Only Temporarily Obscured But truth can be only temporarily obscured. All those noble souls who so unselfishly serve humanity are sure to be rewarded.

It was a sad day for the Christian Church when a man like Origen was disowned. The dark middle ages are a blot on civilization and on Christianity; and it will be a long time before we succeed in recovering the wisdom lost during those centuries of superstition and religious fanaticism. It is a most hopeful sign that the men and women of to-day show themselves unwilling to accept dogmas (such as the doctrine of everlasting punishment) that their parents accepted without question.

*Encyclopædia Britannica, Vol. XVII. p. 839.

Origen Now Coming Into His Own   Origen and other great thinkers of the past are at last coming into their own. It has been said: "You can fool some of the people all of the time, and all of the people some of the time; but not all the people all of the time."

This is a wonderful age in which we are living, and those in the advance guard of humanity who adopt as their motto the axiom that "there is no religion higher than truth," should take every opportunity of studying truth. For the question, What is truth? is uppermost in the minds of men to-day.

His Theological Influence   Although Origen, as has been said, was disowned, no man was actually able to stem the tide of his theological influence.

*"His epoch-making importance lies" in the fact "that all the later parties in the church learned from him. And this is true not only of the dogmatic parties; solitary monks and ambitious priests, hard-headed critical exegetes, allegorists. mystics, all found something congenial in his writings."

How Origen Treated the Scriptures   But what concerns us most is the way in which Origen treated the Scriptures. We are reminded of Philo when we read that Origen maintains his contact with the church by teaching that there are two forms or interpretations of Christianity: namely, the exoteric and the esoteric.

†"This distinction was already current in the catechetical school of Alexandria, but Origen gave it its boldest expression, and justified it on the ground of the incapacity of the Christian masses to grasp the

*Encyclopædia Britannica, Vol. XVII. p. 842.
†Ibid.

deeper sense of Scripture." * * * We read "that the Scriptures * * * are treated by Origen on the basis of matured theory of inspiration in such a way that all their facts appeared as the vehicle of ideas, and have their highest value only in this respect. That is to say, his gnosis neutralizes all that is empirical and historical, if not always as to its actuality, at least absolutely in respect of its value."

His Merit as an Expositor *"Origen's merit as an expositor rests mainly upon the skill and patience with which he evolved the real and natural sense of the Bible. He himself saw clearly that this is the foundation of everything. * * * In relation to his own age, his services are extraordinary."

Origen gives us the key to the whole problem of Biblical interpretation when he teaches that the "facts" contained in the Scriptures are "the vehicles of ideas."

No form of instruction is better fitted to explain an obscure spiritual truth than that of an allegory or parable. Jesus employed no less than ten parables to explain the kingdom of heaven to the uninitiated.

The following statement with regard to Origen and his teaching is highly important, especially as it relates to the present age.

Oracles of Christendom Embrace Ideals of Antiquity †"By proclaiming the reconciliation of science with the Christian faith, of the highest culture with the gospel, Origen did more than any other man to win the Old World to the Christian religion. But he entered into no diplomatic compromises; it was his

---

*The Christian Platonists of Alexandria, by Charles Bigg, D.D., pp. 169, 170.
†Encyclopaedia Britannica, Vol. XVII, p. 839.

deepest and most solemn conviction that the sacred
oracles of Christendom embraced all the ideals of antiquity."

When we learn to interpret the Bible rightly, when
we learn to employ the ancient "key" to unlock the
mysteries of the kingdom, then we shall find, as Origen found, that the science of the present day can be
reconciled with the Christian faith.

**Truth is
Always Truth**   Truth is always truth, no matter on what
plane we search for it. God expresses
Himself in myriad forms and our duty and privilege
is to link up the various manifestations into one beautiful golden chain.

We would agree with Origen that "all the ideals
of antiquity" are embraced in "the sacred oracles of
Christendom."

**All Great
Religions
From The
One Source**   We should remember, however, that a
sharp line of demarcation should be
drawn between certain dogmas in the
Christian Church of to-day and the esoteric or inner phase of primitive Christianity. For,
during the past fifteen-hundred years, certain funda-
mental truths have become almost obliterated. But
when all the great religions of the world are seen to
spring from the One Great Source, then brotherhood
and peace, the dream of all idealists and mystics, will
be an assured fact.

What greater praise can be given a man than this?
*"His character was as transparent as his life was
blameless; there are few church fathers whose biogra-
phy leaves so pure an impression on the reader."

*Encyclopædia Britannica. Vol. XVII. p. 838.

Origen was a great man, and no one can afford to ignore his teachings.

But beware: read, not what unprincipled, biased fanatics have written of him, but his own writings: upon them let your judgment be based.

This advice applies to the works and words of all great teachers and reformers. What the average man believes and has dished up to him day by day, contains as a rule more error than truth.

ST. ATHANASIUS

St. Athanasius is well known owing to the creed that bears his name. The controversy which has centered round this creed shows what a terrible mistake it is to take such utterances literally. There are actually clergymen in the Church of England who refuse to read it, when as a matter of fact, it is most beautiful and instructive if properly translated and interpreted.

By accepting this creed literally, the Church has fallen, to use the words of St. Athanasius, into the most enormous blasphemies; and this acceptance has been literal in spite of this warning that sacred writ should not be interpreted according to the letter.

The Christian Creed The reader is strongly advised to read Mr. C. W. Leadbeater's book entitled The Christian Creed. The writer offers suggestions as to the origin of the three creeds. The Apostles' Creed, the Nicene Creed, and the Athanasian Creed, and expounds them in an original and helpful manner.

*"St. Anthanasius, Bishop of Alexandria, and one

of the most illustrious defenders of the Christian faith, was born at Alexandria about the year 297, (A.D.) * * * It seems certain that Alexander became his patron, took him as a youth into his house, and employed him as his secretary. This was probably about 313, and from this time Athanasius may be said to have been devoted to the Christian ministry."

The Council of Nicæa He was one of the prominent figures in the dispute at the Council of Nicæa in the year 325, and the members of this Council were either bishops or delegates of bishops. In such great esteem was Athanasius held by his contemporaries that he was actually allowed to attend the Council and take part in the discussions, although not a member.

Remarkable Physical and Mental Characteristics *"Theodoret states that 'he contended earnestly for the apostolic doctrines, and was applauded by their champions, while he earned the hostility of their opponents. * * * He * * * is spoken of as remarkable both for his physical and mental charactertistics. He was small in stature, but his face was radiant with intelligence, as "the face of an angel." This is the expression of Gregory of Nazianzus, who has written an elaborate panegyric upon his friend, describing him as fit "to keep on a level with commonplace views, yet also to soar high above the more aspiring," as accessible to all, slow to anger, quick in sympathy, pleasant in conversation, and still more pleasant in temper, effective alike in discourse and in action, assiduous in devotion, helpful to Christians of

*Encyclopædia Britannica, Vol. II. p. 823.

every class and age, a theologian with the speculative, a comforter of the afflicted, a staff to the aged, a guide of the young.

Athanasius Bishop of Alexandria   When his patron and friend Alexander died, Athanasius was elected to be Bishop of Alexandria in his stead, but a few years later, on his refusal to readmit Arius into the Christian communion, he fell under the displeasure of the Emperor Constantine and was banished. When on the death of Constantine he returned to Alexandria "the people ran in crowds to see his face; the churches were full of rejoicing; thanksgivings were offered up everywhere; the ministers and clergy thought the day the happiest in their lives."

But his enemies left him no peace.

Deeply Beloved by His People   Again and again, through the intrigues of the Arian or court party, he was forced to leave the scene of his labours, but always on his return the passionate joy with which he was greeted by his people proved how deeply he was beloved. On the occasion of one of his restorations the people streamed out to meet him, according to Gregory Nazianzus, "like another Nile."

Date of His Death   From the year 366 *"he was left undisturbed to pursue his episcopal labours. Those labours were unceasing in refuting heretics, in building churches, in rebuking rapacious governors, in comforting faithful bishops, and in strengthening the orthodox everywhere, till at length, in the spring of 373, 'in a good old age,' he ceased from all his work.

*Encyclopædia Britannica. Vol. II, pp. 829, 830.

Having consecrated one of his presbyters his successor,
he died quietly in his own house. His 'many struggles,' according to his panegyrists, won him 'many a
crown.' He was gathered to his fathers, patriarchs,
prophets, apostles, and martyrs, who had contended
for the truth. Even those who fail to sympathize with
the cause which Athanasius steadfastly maintained,
cannot refuse their tribute of admiration to his mag-
nanimous and heroic character. * * * If imperious
in temper and inflexible in dogmatic determination,
Athanasius had yet a great heart and intellect, enthu-
siastic in their devotion to Christ, and in work for the
good of the church and of mankind.

His Chief "His chief distinction as a theologian
Distinction as was his zealous advocacy of the essential
a Theologian divinity of Christ as co-equal in substance
with the Father. 'This was the doctrine of the Homoou-
sion, proclaimed by the Nicene Creed, and elaborately
defended by his life and writings. Whether or not
Athanasius first suggested the use of this expression,
he was its greatest defender; and the catholic doctrine
of the Trinity has ever since been more identified with
his 'immortal' name than with any other in the history
of the church and of Christian theology."

ST. GREGORY OF NAZIANZUS

*"St. Gregory of Nazianzus, surnamed Theologus,
one of the four great fathers of the Eastern Church,
was born about the year 329 A.D., at or near Nazianzus, Cappadocia. * * * In the pursuit of a more

*Encyclopædia Britannica, Vol. XI. pp. 179, 180.

liberal and extended culture than could be procured in the insignificant town of Nazianzus, Gregory visited successively the two Cæsareas, Alexandria and Athens, as a student of grammar, mathematics, rhetoric, and philosophy; at the last-named seat of learning, where he prolonged his stay until he had entered his thirtieth year, he enjoyed the society and friendship of Basil, who afterwards became the famous Bishop of Cæsarea. * * * Shortly after his return to his father's house at Nazianzus (about the year 360) Gregory received baptism, and renewed his dedication to the service of religion. * * * Towards 378-379 the small and depressed remnant of the orthodox party in Constantinople sent him an urgent summons to undertake the task of resuscitating the catholic cause, so long persecuted and borne down by the Arians of the Capital. With the accession of Theodosius to the imperial throne, the prospect of success to the Nicene doctrine had dawned, if only it could find some courag-

Gregory a Disciple of Origen and Athanasius

eous and devoted champion. The fame of Gregory as a learned and eloquent disciple of Origen, and still more of Athanasius, pointed him out as such a defender. * * * Once arrived in Constantinople he laboured so zealously and well that the orthodox party speedily gathered strength; and the small apartment in which they had been accustomed to meet was soon exchanged for a vast and celebrated church which received the significant name of Anastasia, the Church of the Resurrection. Among the hearers of Gregory were to be found, not only churchmen like Jerome and Evagrius, but also heretics and heathens; and it says much for the sound wisdom and practical tact of the preacher that from the outset he set himself less to build up and defend a doctrinal position than to urge his flock to the cultivation of the loving Christian spirit which cherishes higher aims than mere heresy hunting or endless disputation." His festival is still celebrated in both the Eastern and Western Churches.

MAIMONIDES

*"Maimonides was born March 30th, 1135 (A.D.), and died at Cairo, December 13, 1204. * * *

Distinguished Talmudist, Mathematician and Astronomer "Like many other great and conscientious Rabbis of all times, who considered it a sin to make of religious learning a means of gaining bread, Maimonides adopted the medical profession. That he must have greatly excelled in it is not merely known by the medical works he composed, but is best testified to by the fact that, although a Jew (and the times and the country he lived in were certainly not more tolerant than ours), he held the lucrative and important office of court-physician to Saladin of Egypt." He was a distinguished Talmudist, and †"a mathematician and astronomer of no mean standing. * * * To sum up in a few words the merits of Maimonides, we may say that, with all the disadvantages of the times in which he lived, he was the greatest theologian and philosopher the Jews ever produced, and one of the greatest the world has seen to this day. As a religious and moral charcater he is equalled only by a few and surpassed by none."

*Encyclopædia Britannica, Vol. XV, p. 295.
†Ibid.

Need we multiply quotations or say more to prove that the Scriptures are allegorical and that we must look beneath the surface if we are to gain the true and spiritual interpretation? All students of the sacred writings can verify the passages cited, if they will take the trouble to study carefully the authorities quoted.

Suffice it to say that the Bible studies which follow deal with the Bible as a "hieroglyph of the soul," as already explained. Thus passages which are utterly meaningless in the literal sense become, when examined as allegories, beautifully clear: indeed they are an inspiration.

If the perusal of these Bible studies will in any way help the reader to love the Bible, the author will feel well repaid.

CHAPTER I.

EVIL DESTROYS ITSELF

The Problem of Evil One of the greatest problems throughout the ages that man has had to face is: What is evil, and how did it originate? If, he argues, God is Good, and God is omnipotent and omnipresent, then Good must be both omnipotent and omnipresent; and if so, there is no room in God or His kingdom for evil. And yet evil is all around us; how are we to account for it?

Searching for the origin of evil is like looking for something that is nothing. Evil is like darkness: God is the divine Light, and it is due to man's ignorance of God that evil exists or is manifested on this plane.

Is Evil Real? The question next arises: Is evil real and has it any true or lasting existence?

The answer is: That if evil is negation, or limitation, or absence of Good, just as darkness is absence of light, then surely it can be considered only as a transitory phenomenon and not a thing that men need fear.

Definitions of Reality Webster says that for a thing to be real it must have "a positive existence." He also gives "truth" as a synonym for "reality." His definition of the word "exist" should also be carefully studied. "Exist," he says, is "to be; to live; to remain; to continue in being."

In Chambers' dictionary we read that "reality" consists of "that which is real and not imaginary."

Nutall states that a thing to be "real" must have "actual being or existence," and to "exist," he says, is "to continue to be."

Jesus said of the devil:

> *"He was a murderer from the beginning, and abode not in the truth, because there is no truth in him. When he speaketh a lie, he speaketh of his own: for he is a liar, and the father of it."

We use the terms, "the world, the flesh and the devil," as terms which signify evil. The Bible also tells us that †"the flesh profiteth nothing."

Evil, then, according to these definitions is: negation, a lie, the absence of truth, ignorance.

We will now apply these definitions to evil and then decide whether it can be considered as a reality, and also whether it has any true existence.

The Definitions Applied
Taking the first word negation, and comparing it with the definition of "real," we see that it is impossible for negation to have "positive existence," since it is not a thing but a want of something.

Again, a lie is not the truth, and truth is a synonym for reality.

And again ignorance, being the absence of knowl-

*St. John. viii :44.
†St. John. vi :63.

edge is negative, not positive. Ignorance is not truth, since wisdom is truth.

Is a lie imaginary or real? And the same question might be asked of negation and ignorance. We might at least say that imaginary could be applied more consistently to a lie, negation, or ignorance, than to truth. A lie does not "continue in being," since the truth destroys it. Ignorance in like manner is destroyed by wisdom.

Evil is a transitory phenomenon, and it is evidently man's duty and privilege to overcome and destroy it: to fear evil is worse than folly. God is not the father of evil, for evil is a lie, and Truth cannot be the father of a lie.

Speaking technically then we are justified from the foregoing in stating that evil is unreal and has no actual being or existence. Just as the want of light is darkness, so the absence of good is evil and the absence of intelligence, non-intelligence.

God is the Only Power Surely then we have ample authority for concluding that God, Good, is the only power, and His law the only law governing the universe; that evil is not a power, and has no law to govern it. And that the only power possessed by evil is the power to destroy itself: apart from this power it is impotent.

In our journey from matter to spirit we rise from plane to plane, ascending the ladder of life round by round; we leave the material and limited beneath our feet, and come nearer and nearer to Spirit, the Unchangeable, the Eternal, the Real. Just to the extent that we are limited, just to that extent are we dwelling in the realm of the unreal.

Is this world limited?

If so, then in proportion to its limitation it is unreal.

*"If we could see all, hear all, touch all, and so forth, there would be no evil, for evil comes of the limitation of perception."

Sin Defined In The Talmud we read:

" 'Sin is an obstruction in the heart; an inability to feel and comprehend all that is noble, true and great, and to take part in the good.' If man is to be freed from sin, his mind and heart must be opened to the influence of enlightenment."

The Story of the Exodus Explained Allegorically We will now apply the key of allegorism to three stories in the Bible, bringing out specially the idea of how evil destroys itself.

The stories chosen are the exodus of the children of Israel from the land of Egypt, the slaying of Goliath by David, and the stilling of the tempest by Jesus, followed by his cure of the demoniac.

Studying the Bible as a "hieroglyph of the soul," we find man's spiritual development described by various allegories. In one of these allegories his development is compared to a journey from Egypt to Jerusalem. Regarding the story from the allegorical point of view, the characters must be considered as thoughts, and the different countries as various states or stages of consciousness in which we sojourn for a period before passing on to a higher or more exalted plane.

*Clothed with the Sun, by Anna Kingsford M.D., p. 88.

Man in Bondage Egypt then is the low material state in which man finds himself in abject slavery to the material senses, to matter and to evil: Jerusalem, where the temple of God stands, is his ultimate destination. The Egyptians are his downward tendencies; Pharaoh their king holds him in a tight grip and forces him to make bricks without straw. The Israelites are the aspiring thoughts in his consciousness: Moses their leader resolves to put an end to this bondage; it is the thought that says: "I am sick unto death of this sin and misery, and by God's help I will find a way out of Egypt: no longer will I be bound down by evil. There is surely a way out of this most difficult situation, and divine Love must and will lead me into a higher state of consciousness, where my fetters will fall away and where the promise of my spiritual birthright will be fulfilled, namely, dominion over the fowl of the air, over the fish of the sea, and over every creeping thing which creepeth upon the earth. Then I shall realize that the kingdom of heaven—the reign of good—is within my soul."

His First Efforts After Freedom According to the Bible story, as soon as Moses made an effort to lead the children of Israel out of Egypt, Pharaoh did his utmost to prevent their departure. And the more Pharaoh tried to hold them back, the more his people were harassed and troubled with plagues and all forms of evil.

The Inner Struggle Undoubtedly we all meet with a similar experience; for there is, to use the terms of Robert Louis Stevenson, a Doctor Jekyl and a Mr. Hyde in each of us, and these two strive together for the mastery. St. Paul refers to this great struggle when he writes:

*"The good that I would I do not: but the evil which I would not, that I do. * * * O wretched man that I am! who shall deliver me from the body of this death?"

So long as we listen to the arguments of Pharoah, so long shall we be held in bondage and be made to suffer.

The Egyptians, stubbornly holding out after enduring nine different plagues, were at last laid low by that terrible calamity, the death of the firstborn.

The story tells us that the Angel of Death, while dealing destruction to every Egyptian household, passed by the houses of the children of Israel, because, in accordance with God's command, they had sprinkled blood "on the two side posts and on the upper door post" of their houses.

Blood Symbolizes Life Now, "blood" throughout the Bible symbolizes life, and in its highest sense the divine life, the Christ Life, which all God's children reflect or manifest to a greater or less degree. That which is good can never die, for in life there is no death, and it is only evil that can be destroyed.

The Start The children of Israel started out fearlessly; but before they had gone far they found the Red Sea stretching in front of them, and the hosts of the Egyptians following them up from behind.

How like our own experience this is! We break

*Romans. vii:19. 24.

away from our state of bondage only to find ourselves in a still worse position. No sooner has one problem been solved than another is staring us in the face. Behind are a host of our old thoughts, fears, habits, appetites, crying wildly after us and pursuing us; before us, a raging sea. But we must not be afraid; we must listen to the words of Moses to the children of Israel:

Fear Not, "Stand Still" *"Fear ye not, stand still, and see the salvation of the Lord, which he will shew to you to day. * * * The Lord shall fight for you, and ye shall hold your peace."

It is essential that we should be fearless from the moment of starting out on this journey; and, paradoxical as it may appear, it is also essential that we should "stand still." For to "stand still" in this sense is not to be stationary in development. It is the stillness of the mind resting in God. Over and over it is stated in the Bible that man must be still; and one significant passage reads: †"Be still, and know that I am God." It is impossible for man really to know anything till he has been able to quiet to a certain extent this raging carnal mind which is likened to a fire, a whirlwind, and an earthquake.

Allegorical Meaning of the Red Sea This Red Sea which now lay spread out before the Israelites is an interesting and fascinating symbol.

It should be noticed in the first instance that this water is sea water, that is, salt water; and in the second that the colour is red. In many of the Bibli-

*Exodus. xiv:13, 14.
†Psalms. xlvi:10.

cal allegories not a single word is to be overlooked if one is to gain the full meaning of the passage. Why then does the writer speak of a Red Sea, and why of a sea at all?

In many passages where Jesus used water as a symbol of life, and in scores of other passages throughout the Bible where the same meaning is intended, it will be observed that fresh water, and not salt, is referred to.

That fresh water was used with this meaning is made quite clear if one will study the story in the New Testament where Jesus is conversing with the woman at the well. The woman told the Master that the well was deep, and that it was impossible for him to draw water from it. But Jesus replied that the water to which he referred was "living water," and that all those who drank of this water should never thirst. This water, which the fresh well water symbolized, was verily the Essence or Substance of Life. For God is Essence, Substance, Life.

Wells of water, rivers of water, still waters, pools of water, springs and brooks, are frequently mentioned in the Bible as symbolic of life; and all of them, be it noticed, are not salt water, but fresh.

Beautiful examples come into one's mind:

*"He leadeth me beside the still waters."
†"He shall drink of the brook in the way: therefore shall he lift up the head."
‡"Therefore with joy shall ye draw water out of the wells of salvation."

*Psalms, xxiii :2.
†Psalms, cx :7.
‡Isaiah, xii :3.

*"And he shewed me a pure river of water of life, clear as crystal, proceeding out of the throne of God and of the Lamb."

The Red Sea on the other hand was salt, and salt was said to have been used amongst the ancient alchemists as a symbol for matter; the Red Sea, therefore, symbolizes a material problem stretching before us.

The second point to be noted is that the Red Sea is not only salt but red.

Those of my readers who have studied physics know that when a ray of light passes through a prism it is immediately broken up into its seven primary colours: red, orange, yellow, green, blue, indigo, violet. We also learn in physics that what appears to the eye to be colour is the result of waves in the ether. These tiny and almost infinitesimal waves have been accurately measured by the physicist. The red is made up roughly of about forty-thousand wave lengths per inch; in other words, it takes about forty-thousand of these little ether waves to produce what we call red: whereas violet, the colour at the other end of the spectrum, is composed of about sixty-thousand wave lengths per inch. Red then is produced by the lowest, and violet by the highest vibrations.

Let us now look at the symbol from the metaphysical point of view.

There are many authorities who declare that every thought has its colour; and they invariably agree that the lower animal thoughts are red, brown and gray in colour; while the higher spiritual thoughts are violet, blue, yellow and pink.

*Revelation. xxii :1

Several of my friends tell me that whenever they give way to temper they actually see red; and we all know that a red flag flaunted in the face of a bull will infuriate him.

This Red Sea, then, stretching before the children of Israel, is a low, animal, materialistic, limited state of consciousness which must be crossed before they can claim to be delivered out of bondage into the glorious liberty of the sons of God.

The Danger of Looking Back Did the children of Israel falter? No. In spite of the obstacle in their path, they trusted in the promise of God, and realized that there would be a way out of this seemingly impossible position. They did not look back as did Lot's wife. She, it will be remembered, looked back longingly on Sodom (which city also symbolizes matter and sensual desires) and was immediately turned into a pillar of salt.

Those of us who, with our past thoughts following us from behind, look back longingly or fearfully upon past experiences will, like Lot's wife, become stationary in matter; in other words, while we encourage these feelings, we shall cease to grow. Many of us indulge in morbid introspection, and this is another form of looking back. There are many other subtle ways in which we revert to the past and make ourselves miserable, remaining day by day, week by week, and year by year in bondage; and this practice is absolutely fatal to spiritual growth.

But if we allow ourselves to be led by the Moses thought, and follow the example of the children of

Israel, moving forward step by step without fear, we, like them, shall be guided by the light by night and by day.

The Pillar of Cloud Here also is another point to be noticed. We read in the nineteenth verse:

*"The pillar of cloud went from before their face, and stood behind them:

"And it came between the camp of the Egyptians and the camp of Israel; and it was a cloud and darkness to them, but it gave light to these."

Here the very same pillar of cloud which was darkness to the Egyptian camp was a source of light to the Israelitish camp.

Evil thoughts and darkness go hand in hand; indeed, evil thoughts are dark thoughts, and no man can expect to be guided by the divine Light so long as he harbours dark thoughts in his consciousness.

Allegorical Meaning of East and West Wind Proceeding with the narrative, we read that the Lord caused a strong east wind to blow all that night, and that this wind †"made the sea dry land, and the waters were divided."

Now this was an east wind that blew, not a west wind; for from the east come all good things.

The sun rises in the east, and one of the most ancient symbols for God is the sun. No better symbol could be chosen, since the physical sun is the light and life of our solar system. David declares: ‡"The Lord God is a sun and shield." And again we read: ‖"But

*Exodus. xiv:19.
†Exodus. xiv:21.
‡Psalms. lxxxiv:11.
‖Malachi. iv:2.

unto you that fear my name shall the sun of righteousness arise with healing in his wings." Jesus said: *"I am the light of the world:" and again it is written, †"In him was life; and the life was the light of men."

So, allegorically, spiritual light comes from the east, and all our spiritual thoughts issue forth from the eastern side of our consciousness.

And just as allegorically all good things come from the east, so all evil things come from the west.

The sun rises in the east, and light is the result; it sets in the west, and darkness follows. Light is associated with life, and darkness with death. Therefore from the east proceeds life, and from the west death.

If we refer back to the nineteenth verse of the tenth chapter of Exodus, we find a significant passage in this connection:

> "And the Lord turned a mighty strong west wind, which took away the locusts, and cast them into the Red Sea; there remained not one locust in all the coasts of Egypt."

Here is an example of how error is self-destroyed. The west wind, symbolizing darkness, error, negation, cast the locusts, symbolizing also error, into the Red Sea, a sea of error, where they were destroyed.

> "O error, soon conceived,
> Thou never com'st unto a happy birth
> But kill'st the mother that engendered thee."

The east wind here might be taken as a symbol of the divine breath of life, of life-giving thoughts, spiritual thoughts or pure thoughts. It is this type of

*St. John. viii:12.
†St. John. 1:4.

thought that separates the red salt waters and allows the pilgrim to proceed on his way.

Divine Intelligence Destroys Ignorance How encouraging it is to know that if we go calmly and fearlessly on our journey, this seemingly terrible problem will disappear like darkness before the light! It must disappear. For evil is nothing but ignorance; and how can ignorance stand beside divine Intelligence? Our duty is "to know the truth," to reflect or express divine Intelligence in every thought, word and action: then it is that the so-called impossible can be achieved.

Monotheism vs. Dualism Those who are afraid of the Red Sea are giving power to evil; they are looking upon it as a reality, and as an actual force opposed to good: they are dualists, not monotheists. So long as we believe in two powers, we shall never succeed. St. James tells us that *"a double minded man is unstable in all his ways," and Jesus says, †"If * * * thine eye be single, thy whole body shall be full of light."

Let us now follow the fate of the Egyptians.

Evil Destroys Itself There is an old saying that if you give a fool rope enough he will hang himself. Evil is like this foolish man, for given enough rope it will surely destroy itself. We remember what became of the locusts; the same fate overtook the Egyptians. They saw the children of Israel pass safely over on dry ground to the other side of the Red Sea, and they pursued them, imagining that where the children of Israel went they too might go. Evil is always shortsighted;

*St. James. 1:8.
†St. Matthew, vi:22.

it must be so, since it has no spiritual insight—no inner perception. No sooner were the Egyptians in the bed of the sea than *"the waters returned and covered the chariots, and the horsemen, and all the host of Pharaoh that came into the sea after them; there remained not so much as one of them. * * * And Israel saw the Egyptians dead upon the sea shore."

There is a great lesson to be learned from this story. The powerful host of the Egyptians, or shall we say the seemingly powerful host, for we must remember that the Egyptians symbolize the evil or limited thoughts in our consciousness, were utterly and absolutely destroyed. There is but one thing to fear as far as evil is concerned, and that is our fear of evil; but "perfect love"—the love of God—"casteth out fear." We must keep our eyes steadfastly fixed on the good, our star; and thus we are sure to be guided aright.

David's Conquest Over Goliath Another instance of evil destroying itself is given in the fascinating story of David's fight with Goliath. This story is a fine example of how the Scriptures are illuminated when we interpret them spiritually instead of taking them literally. The narrative is found in the seventeenth chapter of the first book of Samuel, and every sentence of it is full of meaning.

Before describing the battle, it will be well to make a careful study of the two leading characters, David and Goliath.

The Meaning of David Christ is often spoken of as the son of David, and the Scriptures tell us that we must have that mind in us that was also

‡Exodus. xiv:28, 30.

in Christ Jesus.   What then is the meaning of the word **David**?

Gerald Massey in his **Book of the Beginnings,** says that the Egyptian word **Taht** is synonymous with Hermes, and what is even more significant, that *"David is the Hebrew Hermes or Taht."

An account of Hermes is given by James Drummond in **Philo Judaeus** ,as follows:

†"Hermes is reason, the Logos whom the gods sent to us out of heaven. * * *   He carries winged sandals in agreement with Homer's 'winged words.' He is fabled to be the conductor of souls, * * *   and he is furnished with a rod wherewith he soothes the eyes of men, and, again, wakes those that sleep. * * *   The serpents twined about his herald's rod symbolize his power of charming the brutal. * * *   His parents were represented as Zeus and Maia."

The following passage is also worthy of notice:

‡"Jamblichus * * *   makes the remark that Hermes the god of learning and language was formerly considered as the common property of the priests, and the power who presides over the true science concerning the ‡gods, is one and the same universally."

*A Book of the Beginnings, by Gerald Massey. Vol. II.

†Philo Judaeus, by James Drummond, LL. D., Vol. I, pp. 122-3.

‡The word "gods" is usually misunderstood by the average reader. The ancient Egyptians were monotheists. Their gods were attributes of the One God, the First Great Cause, the Absolute.

For example:

Ra, the Sun God, is "the lord of heaven, the Prince (Life, Health, Strength!), the Creator of the gods." (The Book of the Dead, Vol. I, p. 5.)

Khepera—"He is a form of the rising sun, and his seat is in the boat of the Sun-god. He is the god of matter which is on the point of passing from inertness into life, and also of the dead body from which a spiritual and glorified body is about to burst forth. His emblem is a beetle." (Ibid. Vol. I, p. 4.)

Thoth—"The divine intelligence which at the creation uttered the words which resulted in the formation of the world. He was self-produced, and was lord of earth, air, sea and sky; he was the scribe of the gods, and the inventor of all arts and sciences." (Ibid. Vol. I, p. 5.)

Maat—"The wife of Thoth, and daughter of Ra; she assisted at the work of crea-

In an invocation to Hermes the following expression is used, "the good mind."

From the above we gather that David, Hermes or Taht symbolically is the good Mind, Reason, the Logos or Word of God; "the power who presides over the true science"; the winged messenger of Truth and Love, who wakes sleepy mortals, giving them spiritual perception, and charming or transmuting the brutal, animal nature.

"The name of David or Dud," Gerald Massey goes on to say, "has the same significations as that of Taht. Tut means to unite, engender, establish; Dud, to unite, join together, bind, make fast, or establish. Taht is the servant of Ra, Dud is the servant of Jah. The genealogy also tends to show their identity."

In the light of this citation, a man is a David when he is a servant of God (Ra or Jah), when he is united or joined with divine Intelligence, and when he is made fast and established.

Christ the Son of David It is now quite clear why Jesus the Christ is spoken of as the Son of David. Christ is, in fact, the Son of the Good Mind, or that one mind

---

tion. She is the goddess of absolute regularity and order, and of moral rectitude, and of right and truth. Her emblem is the feather." (Ibid. Vol. I. p. 4.)

Osiris—"The god who after death and mutilation upon earth rose again and became the king of the underworld and judge of the dead; he was the type of eternal existence, and the symbol of immortality. The deceased pleads the resurrection of this god as the reason for his own resurrection, and he always identifies himself with Osiris in funeral rites." (Ibid. Vol. I. p. 4.)

Isis—"The heart of the Lady of Life." (Ibid. Vol. I. p. 8.)

The Christian is not accused of being a polytheist when he refers to God at one time as Life, and at another as Love. To have many names or attributes for God is not to be an idolator. The ancient Chinese, Hindus, Buddhists and Zoroastrians were also monotheists. The ignorant in all ages, including the present, have misunderstood the inner or real Truth embodied in the great religions of the world; and this misunderstanding has been the chief reason for our calling the devotees of the ancient religions heathen.

which presides over the true science of the universe.
There can be but one Mind, and therefore but one
science. God's law is the only law, and this "law of
the spirit of life in Christ Jesus," sets man free from
the "law of sin and death." This is the power which
is to fight and conquer Goliath. And to conclude, we
are Davids when we express or reflect divine Intelligence, the one Mind.

Another
Aspect
of David
Another aspect of David, and one which
must not be ignored, is beautifully explained by Mr. Maitland. He tells us that
in our journey from Egypt to Jerusalem there is a
point which we might call the "half-way house:" this,
he says, is specially conspicuous in the Bible.

*"This is the stage represented by 'David.'" *
* * He is "the type of the man who, being but
partially regenerate, is liable to oscillate between the
two extremes of his nature, ascending under the influence of his regenerated part to the heights of spiritual perception and divine communion; and, under the
influence of his still unregenerate part, descending to
the depths of sensuality and cruelty. Nevertheless,
the regenerative or Christ-process, has begun in him,
in due time to be completed."

All of us to-day are more or less in the position of
David.

Goliath
Defined
Who then is Goliath?
He is the archenemy of the soul, a ver-
itable giant and the chief of the Philistines. He rep-
resents "that system of doubt and denial which finds

*The Bible's Own Account of Itself, by Edward Maitland. B. A., p. 43.

its inevitable outcome in materialism." In the fight between Goliath and David, we see the fight of materialism against the inner spiritual understanding.

David's Earlier Achievements Let us return to David for a moment and look at his earlier achievements. To prove to Saul that he was able to overcome Goliath, he related that once, when a lion and a bear had attacked his father's sheep, he had been enabled to slay them both. In like manner we must all kill the lions and the bears in our consciousness before we attempt to fight the great Goliath.

The Four Beasts, and the Son of Man Daniel's vision of the four beasts throws light on this subject:

*"And four great beasts came up from the sea, diverse one from another.

"The first was like a lion, and had eagle's wings: * * *

"And behold another beast, a second, like to a bear."

It will be noticed that there were four of these beasts. The number four in this connection is symbolical of the lower, animal, materialistic, four-sided nature of man. It is most illuminating to find that these four beasts came up, not from fresh water, but from the sea, since they are material or salt manifestations. The lion and the bear which David killed are symbolically identical with those mentioned by Daniel, for we go on to read that the thrones of the four beasts were cast down.

*Daniel. vii:3-5.

*"I beheld then because of the voice of the great words which the horn spake: I beheld even till the beast was slain, and his body destroyed, and given to the burning flame.

"As concerning the rest of the beasts, they had their dominion taken away: yet their lives were prolonged for a season and time.

"I saw in the night visions, and, behold one like the Son of man came with the clouds of heaven, and came to the Ancient of days, and they brought him near before him.

"And there was given him dominion, and glory, and a kingdom, that all people, nations, and languages, should serve him: his dominion is an everlasting dominion, which shall not pass away, and his kingdom that which shall not be destroyed."

We see here that the Son of man which is no other than the Son of David—Christ, the Christ within us, eventually gains dominion over all the earth, or over all the animal, materialistic thoughts in our consciousness.

A Glorious Fight This great work, however, must be accomplished by degrees. We cannot rise to divine heights until we have killed Goliath: we have not even killed the lions and the bears in our consciousness while we are still apt to lose our temper, to be resentful, or consumed with the fires of jealousy. There is no bed of roses for the Christian knight: his life is a battle. But it is a glorious fight, not a hopeless struggle. If we begin aright, putting absolute

*Daniel, vii:11-14.

faith in the good, and fearlessly set ourselves to overcome the animal thoughts, desires and passions in our lower nature, symbolized by Daniel's four beasts, we assuredly shall gain that dominion and glory, that everlasting dominion which shall not pass away.

David the David was a shepherd, and we like Da-
Shepherd Boy vid are all shepherds; but do we tend our wandering sheep? For our thoughts, like sheep, are prone to wander. Therefore, watchfulness and self-control are essential. We must be careful not to leave the door of the sheepfold open; otherwise the lion and the bear may steal in unawares and snatch away the beautiful thought which we have been cherishing. Christ is the door of the sheepfold. If we let the Christ within us *"stand porter at the door of thought," we shall suffer no loss from the ravages of our foes.

Another thought that must be borne in mind with regard to David is that during the years that he was tending his sheep, he was practicing with his sling. The Christian warrior must also become an adept in throwing stones if he expects to strike Goliath in the vital spot.

Let us now turn to the story.

Goliath's A subtle temptation came to David
Armour through Saul the material king, who endeavored to persuade him to wear armour similar to that which Goliath was wearing.

It behooves us to make a careful study of Goliath's armour. The story tells us that he wore a helmet of brass upon his head, greaves of brass upon his legs,

*Science and Health, by Mary Baker G. Eddy, p. 392.

and a target of brass between his shoulders. The weight of his coat of mail was five thousand shekels of brass, and his spear's head weighed six hundred shekels of iron.

Brass here indicates the sensual thoughts, while iron typifies the human or carnal will-power. It will be noticed that the weight of his spear's head was six hundred shekels of iron. Now, whenever we find six, or multiples of six, in the Bible it usually signifies toil, sin, and suffering for sin. Surely it is the experience of all of us, that whenever we employ evil thoughts or animal will-power, we always come to grief. A spear pointed with animal or will-power is of no value in the battle of life. Goliath's coat of mail weighed five thousand shekels of brass. The number five indicates the fivefold nature of man. We have five senses, five extremities, five fingers on each hand, five toes on each foot. So the number five is aptly chosen.

The Armour of Materialism Does Not Fit the Warrior of God Now David was invited by Saul to wear armour of this description; and from the material point of view, nothing could have been more reasonable than to fight this eleven-foot giant—he was six cubits and a span in height—clad in similar armour. But David was not to be led away by material arguments, the subtle wisdom of the carnal mind which Solomon declares is vanity. David explained to Saul that he had not proved this armour; and, confident that as he had been delivered from the paw of the lion and the paw of the bear, he would also be delivered from the hand of the Philistine, he went to meet his foe with nothing but a staff and a sling in his hand.

The great Goliath laughed him to scorn, and boasted that he would give his flesh to the fowls of the air and to the beasts of the field; but David calmly walked down to the brook and chose from it five smooth stones.

The Water of Life This brook out which the stones were chosen typifies the water of life previously referred to. This water is the true Substance or Spirit from which all good thoughts proceed, and the stones represent good thoughts, which good thoughts are things, since God or Mind is Substance.

Five Stones Are Essential It is interesting to note that the number of stones David chose was five. Now in order to conquer our five-pointed sensual nature, we must not appear on the battle field with only one, two, three, or four stones; nothing short of five will suffice. For man has five senses: taste, sight, touch, smell and hearing. Let us suppose that he attempts one morning to go through the day with only four stones: taste has no temptation for him, the lust of the eye has no fears, the pleasures of the senses associated with touch are conquered, and the enticements connected with the olfactory nerves are put aside with disdain. But since he has left his fifth stone behind, he finds himself, when least aware of it, listening to some spicy scandal. His enemy Goliath has attacked him at his weak spot, and has conquered him.

David, however, was well prepared; and when the giant arose and came to meet him, David ran, and with unerring precision slung one of his stones at the giant, so that the stone sank into his forehead, and he fell upon his face to the earth.

*"So David prevailed over the Philistine with a sling and with a stone, and smote the Philistine, and slew him; but there was no sword in the hand of David."

Never Fight Error with the Weapons of Error Notice particularly that last sentence. It is never possible for us to overcome evil with evil. In the New Testament it is explicitly stated: †"Be not overcome of evil, but overcome evil with good." Never fight error with its own weapons, for by so doing you are sure to fail.

Jesus declared:

‡All they that take the sword shall perish with the sword."

We are further commanded to love our enemies, to bless them that curse us, and to pray for those that persecute us. This may seem a difficult task, but it is the only safe course to pursue. God is omnipotent, and good thoughts are sure to bring us out victorious in the end.

Strike in the Right Place The reader should also notice that the stone struck Goliath in the forehead. Phrenologists tell us that perception is located in this portion of the brain. It is well for us to remind ourselves that the brain is not the mind, but the instru-

*I Samuel, xvii:50.
†Romans, xii:21.
‡St. Matthew, xxvi:52.

ment of the mind. The forehead then is that portion of the brain through which perception is expressed or manifested. Now, evil claims to be very wise, but its wisdom is only the wisdom of this world. The serpent which crawls in the dust tries to persuade man that material wisdom is all-sufficient; but divine Wisdom must eventually displace the material sense of life. This material sense of life is really negation, or ignorance of good. When the stone of truth strikes this weak spot, the giant Goliath, who seems to have such marvelous power, falls to the earth. Evil is a bully, a boaster masquerading as a great giant with enormous power; but the Christian warrior need have no fear: if we dwell *" in the secret place of the most High," we "shall abide under the shadow of the Almighty."

The lion and the bear are trampled under foot; a thousand may fall at our side, and ten thousand at our right hand, but no harm can befall us.

The most interesting part of the story is yet to follow.

Evil a Disintegrating Destructive Force   David, after Goliath has fallen to the earth, rushes forward and cuts off his head. He uses the very sword with which he himself, according to his enemy's boast, was to have been slain.

There is an old saying that curses, like chickens, come home to roost. Evil has but one power, and that power is the power to destroy itself: otherwise it is impotent. The Christian must always realize that evil and evil thoughts, like chickens, return to roost

*Psalms, xci :1.

in the consciousness of the evil thinker only to come to nothing in the end.

We must, however, in this allegorical statement, distinguish between the man himself, and the evil thoughts in his consciousness. It is not man who is to be destroyed, but the ignorance in the consciousness of man. It is unthinkable that the Creator, the all-wise, beneficent Father-Mother-God, should create a man only to destroy him: universal salvation is the only logical conclusion to be reached by any student. Man must be saved because he is the image and likeness of God, Good; and that which is good cannot be destroyed.

The great Goliath, therefore, which wars against man, is man's ignorant, sensual, materialistic sense of life. As man's spiritual consciousness is unfolded, so his lower nature is "put off," and the new man in Christ Jesus is "put on." It is then that his materialistic sense of life falls away into nothingness from whence it came.

How glorious and inspiring it is to feel and know that evil is negation! For this knowledge we must all thank God, and take courage.

The Allegorical Meaning of the Stilling of the Tempest and the Cure of the Demoniac We now come to the third story—that of Christ stilling the tempest and curing the demoniac.

The story is related by St. Matthew, St. Mark and St. Luke. St. Matthew speaks of two demoniacs while the others speak of one. But this difference in detail makes no difference to the meaning underlying the story

The external discrepancy is of no moment: the internal harmony is all important.

To outline the story briefly:

*Jesus was crossing the lake with his disciples when a storm arose. The disciples, filled with fears, aroused him, for he had fallen asleep, and besought him to save them. Jesus reproached them for their fears, and calmed the winds and the waves.

Landed on the other side, Jesus was met by a demoniac, who said his name was Legion, for he was possessed by many devils. Jesus commanded the devils to depart from the man, and they besought him to allow them to enter into a herd of swine feeding near the mountains. He suffered them, and the whole herd rushed down a steep place into the sea, and were drowned.

Professor Huxley's Criticism This story has been a happy hunting ground for the higher critics. Professor Huxley was exceedingly annoyed at this passage, and in his book of essays, entitled **Science and Christian Tradition**, he says:

†"I think it may be granted that the people whose herd of 2,000 swine (more or fewer) was suddenly destroyed suffered great loss and damage. * * *

"Any one who acted in the way described in the story would, in my judgment, be guilty of 'a misdemeanor of evil example.'

"I leave no shadow of doubt as to my own choice: 'after what has been said, I do not think that any sensible man, unless he happen to be angry, will accuse me of "contradicting the Lord and his Apostles" if I re-

*St. Mark. iv:35-41. Chapter v:1-20.
†Science and Christian Tradition, by Thomas H. Huxley, pp. 369-371.

iterate my total disbelief in the whole Gadarene story.' "

Futile Arguments The above statement appeared in a reply to an article by Mr. Gladstone, and it is certainly most pathetic to see two great men like Professor Huxley and Mr. Gladstone arguing over this narrative in such a futile and childish manner. Both were wrong in their conclusions, and this unseemly controversy would never have occurred if they had understood that the whole story is a beautiful allegory.

It is interesting to refer to a few more passages from **Science and Christian Tradition,** for they show to what lengths people will go in trying to prove some pet theory.

Professor Huxley writes:

Mr. Gladstone's Statement *"I am afraid, therefore, that Mr. Gladstone must have been exceedingly angry when he committed himself to such a statement as follows:

" 'So, then, after eighteen centuries of worship offered to our Lord by the most cultivated, the most developed, and the most progressive portion of the human race, it has been reserved to a scientific enquirer to discover that He (Christ) was no better than a law-breaker and evil-doer. * * * How, in such a matter, came the honours of originality to be reserved to our time and to Professor Huxley?' "

Ludicrous but Serious Incidents "Truly," says Professor Huxley, "the hatchet is hardly a weapon of precision, but would seem to have rather more the

*Ibid. pp. 371-2.

character of the boomerang, which returns to damage the reckless thrower. Doubtless such incidents are somewhat ludicrous. But they have a very serious side."

It might be mentioned that Mr. Gladstone was endeavoring to prove that the province where the swine were drowned was under the jurisdiction of the Jews, and, therefore, it would be unlawful for the people to raise swine; and this being the case, it was perfectly legitimate for Jesus to allow them to be drowned. Professor Huxley proved that Mr. Gladstone was wrong in his contention, for he states,

*"The proof that Gadara was, to all intents and purposes, a Gentile, and not a Jewish, city is complete. The date and occasion of its foundation are unknown; but it certainly existed in the third century B.C. Antiochus the Great annexed it to his dominions in B.C. 198."

Professor Huxley then goes to great pains to give a full history of this part of the country for hundreds of years, and all to no purpose.

The Myth of the Creation These critics made an equally sad spectacle of themselves, during the controversy over the great Pentateuchal myth of the creation. Professor Huxley in speaking of Mr. Gladstone on this occasion writes:

†"Mr. Gladstone's manifest want of acquaintance with the facts and principles involved in the discussion, no less than with the best literature on his own side of the subject, gave me the uncomfortable feeling that

*Ibid. p. 379.
†Ibid. p. 367.

I had my adversary at a disadvantage. The sun of science, at my back, was in his eyes."

And again:

Moses and the Pentateuch *"Only one point became perfectly clear to me, namely, that Moses is not responsible for nine-tenths of the Pentateuch; certainly not for the legends which had been made the bugbears of science. In fact, the fence turned out to be a mere heap of dry sticks and brushwood, and one might walk through it with impunity: the which I did."

The fence referred to by Professor Huxley was a †"thorny barrier with its comminatory notice-board—'No Thoroughfare. By order. Moses.' " He further states with regard to this barrier: ‡"I had set out on a journey, with no other purpose than that of exploring a certain province of natural knowledge; I strayed no hair's breadth from the course which it was my right and my duty to pursue." He then goes on to say that no matter what route he took he shortly came to a "formidable-looking fence." So he proceeded to knock down what he called "a mere heap of ruins; venerable, indeed, and archæologically interesting, but of no other moment."

Exhibitions of Ignorance Professor Huxley little dreamed that the Pentateuch is not to be judged from a scientific point of view. Such exhibitions of ignorance are not only sad, but astounding in this enlightened age, and especially when there is so much literature at the disposal of the unprejudiced investigator. It is most unfortunate, however, to note that men of this

* Ibid. Preface. IX.
†Ibid. Preface. VIII.
‡Ibid. Preface. VII.

type are on many points very narrow minded and shortsighted, in fact dogmatic, for it is quite as possible to be dogmatic in matters connected with science as in religion. I say an exhibition of this kind is sad, because these men were honest and sincere. Professor Huxley himself states:

Professor Huxley's Defence *"I distinctly decline to admit some of the items charged; more particularly that of having 'gone out of my way' to attack the Bible; and I as steadfastly deny that 'hatred of Christianity' is a feeling with which I have any acquaintance. There are very few things which I find it permissible to hate; and though, it may be, that some of the organizations, which arrogate to themselves the Christian name, have richly earned a place in the category of hateful things, that ought to have nothing to do with one's estimation of the religion, which they have perverted and disfigured out of all likeness to the original." And yet poor Professor Huxley is perverting and disfiguring it just as much by applying his scientific method of criticism.

Many scholars have wondered why Jesus should have been the indirect means of drowning the swine.

This narrative, like the others, has an allegorical or spiritual interpretation, and when looked at from this standpoint is full of meaning.

Stillness is Necessary to Knowledge The first thing to be noted is that Jesus stilled the tempest so that there was a great calm, and that he dispelled the fears of the disciples.

*Ibid. Preface VII.

Each of us must realize that the Christ within us is the hope of our salvation. This Christ it is that stills the tempest of the carnal mind, and dispels our fears; and we can never hope to cast out these devils which are the evil thoughts in our consciousness, until we are still, and until we are free from fear. Neither, till we are still, can we know the truth or hear the inner spiritual voice.

The Meaning of Swine We will now consider the meaning of the swine. Among the Jews these animals were the symbol of everything that was unclean.

> *"Give not that which is holy unto the dogs, neither cast ye your pearls before swine, lest they trample them under their feet, and turn again and rend you."

Evil Attracts Evil The prodigal son, it will be remembered, when he had wandered far from his father's house and had spent all his substance in riotous living, †"would fain have filled his belly with the husks that the swine did eat." In watching a pig we notice how it delights to wallow in the mire, and what an unclean feeder it is. In every way it is a symbol of that which is unclean—a symbol of evil. These swine were therefore a channel for evil, in other words, they attracted the evil or the devils which were cast out of the demoniac. We are all familiar with the saying, "Birds of a feather flock together." Evil attracts evil; and if we do not wish to be what the world calls unlucky, we should be careful not to harbour evil

*St. Matthew. vii:6.
†St. Luke. xv:16.

or unclean thoughts. It is dangerous to feed on swinish thoughts, for evil seeks the channel of least resistance.

All Evil to be Destroyed We now come to the final and most interesting part of the whole story: the possessed swine rushed headlong down a steep place into the sea, also typical of evil, and were drowned. They met their death in identically the same manner as the Egyptians. Material thoughts are only fit to be destroyed. The same type of thought or carnal mind which held the children of Israel in bondage, also bound with chains this demoniac.

In the presence of Christ, however, they were impotent.

So, as the Christ-idea grows in us, it will drive out all error, and then we shall be able to sing with St. John the Divine:

> *"I saw a new heaven and a new earth: for the first heaven and the first earth were passed away; and there was no more sea.
>
> . . . .
>
> "And God shall wipe away all tears from their eyes; and there shall be no more death, neither sorrow, nor crying, neither shall there be any more pain: for the former things are passed away."

*Revelation. xxi :1, 4.

CHAPTER II.

LOVE THE FULFILLING OF THE LAW

The Word Love There is probably no word in the English language more grossly misunderstood or misused than this little word of four letters, love. Speaking casually, we might say that it is one of the easiest words to define: when we give the matter deeper consideration, we discover that there is probably no word more difficult to define. For we come to see that love is, in its highest sense, God. And who can fathom infinity?

Love the Feminine Aspect of Deity The more we study this word, the more we discern how much it embraces. Viewing it in its highest sense, we might say that love is synonymous with the Mother-God, the Universal Soul or Substance, the matrix or womb in which the universe is evolved or nurtured. It is the feminine aspect of Deity; and God as the divine Mother, sacrifices the very essence of Soul that the universe may come into being, and that man may enjoy all that is beautiful and good in it.

Love is Law or Principle St. Paul says that *"love is the fulfilling of the law."

This truth is not evident at first sight; but the

*Romans, xiii:10.

more we study the Scriptures, observe our fellow men
and investigate in turn the various laws and phenom-
ena with which we come in contact on this physical
plane, the more deeply are we persuaded, not only that
love is the fulfilling of the law, but that love is the
Law or Principle in its very essence.

**Man is
Feminine
as well as
Masculine.** We have said that this word in its highest aspect is the Mother-God. In man,
the microcosm, we have this same feminine aspect, principle or quality—the
woman in man. For if man is the image and likeness
of God, he must in the absolute or true sense be the
image and likeness of the Father-Mother-God: therefore he is feminine as well as masculine.

Perhaps before we go further we ought to explain
that the word **man** when used in this sense includes
both sexes, just as the word mankind does.

**The Word
Woman** This point being understood, it is interesting to note that the word **woman** is
used throughout the Bible to represent allegorically
this feminine principle or aspect of man. In the second
chapter of the book of Genesis we read that the seed
of the woman shall bruise the serpent's head; and all
through the Scriptures, book by book, we find this
same woman until we come to the book of Revelation,
where she is referred to as *"a woman clothed with the
sun."

**The Twofold
Meaning
of Woman** This word **woman**, like so many other
words, has a twofold meaning. In its
first meaning, woman represents the sen-

*Revelation. xii:1.

sual, animal nature which enslaves man and drags him down into the dust, and as such is the inverted or perverted sense of woman. For in this respect, the woman, or soul, or intuitive sense, in the early stages of man's development, is subject to the human will: the woman, in other words, is subject to the man. And she is so because she has not been sufficiently awakened. This higher spiritual sense lies dormant within the soul. Man being only partially awake cannot hear the "still small voice" of divine Love. The outer tumult of the animal or carnal mind downs the voice of this angel visitant.

In its second and higher meaning, woman symbolizes the noblest, purest and best qualities in man's innermost nature; at a higher stage of man's development, she is no longer subject to the human will; but as spiritual intuition, guides man onward and upward in his journey from earth to heaven.

The Woman Who Was a Sinner A study of the beautiful story in the gospels, recorded of the woman who anointed Jesus' feet, may help us to understand this idea.

We read that when Jesus was at meat at the house of a certain Pharisee, Simon by name, a woman who was a sinner brought an alabaster box.

*"And stood at his feet behind him weeping, and began to wash his feet with tears, and did wipe them with the hairs of her head, and kissed his feet, and anointed them with the ointment." Whereupon Simon said to himself:

*St. Luke, vii:38.

The Man Who Was a Pharisee *"This man, if he were a prophet, would have known who and what manner of woman this is that toucheth him: for she is a sinner."

This pharisaical thought must give birth to many other undesirable thoughts and deeds; otherwise it is not deserving of so sweeping a condemnation as that pronounced upon it by the Christ.

A Pharisee is blind, selfish and cruel. Everything becomes perverted when observed through his self-righteous glasses. He is devoid of love, sympathy, gentleness and compassion. That he must become as a little child before he can possibly enter the kingdom of heaven is Greek to him. The giant of selfishness is his master. He little realizes that we must sacrifice our life to gain life eternal. He suffers from "exaggerated ego," and his sins of omission are as numerous as his sins of commission. Lacking love, he cannot understand what Christian service and charity mean. Seemingly rich, he is in reality poor; a man to be pitied, not envied. Jesus referred to the man who harboured self-righteous thought as a whited sepulchre filled with dead men's bones.

The Contrast What a difference there was between this self-righteous thought of Simon, and the self-sacrificing, loving, grateful thought of the woman! The anointing of Jesus' feet filled her with joy. She thought nothing of what she was to receive: she thought only of what she could give. So overwhelming was her gratitude that she felt her costly gift to be no sacrifice: it was the outpouring of her very soul. She loved

*St. Luke vii: 39.

the Christ, loved him from the very depths of her being; and as she now saw the beauty of this divine or Christ idea, she turned away with sorrow and repentance from her former life.

Ingersoll's Eulogy   Could this self-sacrificing love be better described than in the following words of Robert G. Ingersoll:

"The one thing in this world that is constant, the one window in which light forever burns, the one star which darkness cannot quench, is woman's love. It rises to the greatest height; it sinks to the lowest depth; it forgives the most cruel injuries. It is perennial of life and grows in any climate; neither coldness nor neglect, harshness nor cruelty can extinguish it. A woman's love is the perfume of the heart. This is the real love that wrought miracles in art; that gives music all the way from the cradle song to the symphony that bears the soul away on wings of fire: a love that is greater than power, sweeter than life, and stronger than death."

But the reader may ask what this has to do with love being the fulfilling of the law.

The Bible is "a Hieroglyph of the Soul"   It must be remembered that the Bible is "a hieroglyph of the soul," so let us try to realize that within our consciousness there are two types of thought: the pharisaical type and the Mary Magdalene, each being the antithesis of the other, and each striving to master the other. The Christ idea is also within us, for the kingdom of heaven or God is within us. St. Paul speaks of "Christ in you, the hope of glory." In the narrative we find that the

Pharisee was condemned, whereas the Magdalen was blessed and forgiven, for it is only through giving that we receive.

St. Paul's Love-Song   Let us now turn to the thirteenth chapter of the first epistle to the Corinthians, where we find one of the most beautiful definitions of love. We shall summarize this definition, and then compare it with Mary's act of devotion and gratitude.

St. Paul begins by telling us that although we may "have the gift of prophecy, and understand all mysteries, and all knowledge;" though we have faith to remove mountains, and yet lack love, we are nothing. All these gifts devoid of love are impotent and useless.

But what is St. Paul's definition of love?

He tells us that love is free from envy and self-righteousness or pride, and that it "thinketh no evil," "seeketh not her own, is not easily provoked," and "rejoiceth in the truth." Love "hopeth all things, endureth all things," and "never faileth."

If a man made love, as defined by St. Paul, the law of his life, he would be transformed. Mary in her act expressed much that is spoken of here. Jesus therefore said of her that her many sins were forgiven her because she loved much.

In the study of this story it would be well for the reader to refer to the other gospels, which give rather different versions, throwing side lights upon it.

The Judas Iscariot Thought   In the account given in St. John's gospel, *Judas Iscariot, the purse bearer of the little company, asked why the ointment had not been "sold for three-hundred pence, and given

*St. John, xii:1-9.

to the poor;" and he asked this "because he was a thief, and had the bag, and bare what was put therein."

The Judas Iscariot thought in our consciousness is the grasping, self-seeking thought: it is the thought that betrays the Christ. Before we can gain the faintest idea of the meaning of love, we must forget self. We, like Mary, must recognize the Christ idea in our consciousness. We must not only recognize it, but love it and be willing to give up all if necessary for it. So long as we cling to the treasures of earth instead of looking within for this Christ idea, just so long shall we grovel in the dust of materialism and betray and crucify the Christ. We must cultivate the Mary thought; otherwise the Simon and Judas thoughts will gain the ascendency.

Love is Life In the first epistle of St. John we find this passage:

> *"We know that we have passed from death unto life, because we love the brethren. He that loveth not his brother abideth in death.
>
> "Whosoever hateth his brother is a murderer: and ye know that no murderer hath eternal life abiding in him."

It has been said: "Nothing else is necessary but this: love, sincerity, and patience. What is life but growth, i.e. expansion; i.e. love. Therefore all love is life, it is **the only law of life**; all selfishness is death, and this is true here or hereafter."

Love is Light We also find that this love is Light, for we read in the first epistle of St. John:

*I John iii:14. 15.

*"He that loveth his brother abideth in the light, and there is none occasion of stumbling in him.

"But he that hateth his brother is in darkness, and walketh in darkness, and knoweth not whither he goeth, because that darkness hath blinded his eyes."

Love is Faithful Love then is Life and Light, and casts out all fear. It is most interesting to observe how the women were faithful to Christ to the end. During his agony in the garden of Gethsemane, his most trusted disciples slept. When he was surrounded and taken by the band of men and officers from the chief priests, his disciples forsook him and fled. While he was being tried before Caiaphas, Peter denied him thrice. It is therefore a great relief to notice in St. Matthew's gospel that when he was on the cross

†"Many women were there beholding afar off, which followed Jesus from Galilee, ministering unto him:

"Among which was Mary Magdalene, and Mary the mother of James and Joses, and the mother of Zebedee's children."

According to St. John, they were even at the foot of the cross; and with them John himself, the disciple whom Jesus loved.

The women followed to the sepulchre and ‡"beheld where he was laid." And when Joseph of Arimathæa had buried the body of Jesus, and had rolled a

*I John, iii:10, 11.
†St. Matthew, xxvii:55, 56.
‡St. Mark, xv:47.

great stone to the door of the sepulchre and had departed, *"there was Mary Magdalene, and the other Mary, sitting over against the sepulchre."

Love is Fearless and is Always Rewarded   Real spiritual love is true unto death, and knows no fear. And it is inspiring to note that such love is always rewarded, although reward is neither sought for nor expected.

Those who were last at the cross were first also at the tomb of the risen Christ.

†"The first day of the week cometh Mary Magdalene early, when it was yet dark, unto the sepulchre, and seeth the stone taken away from the sepulchre.

"Then she runneth, and cometh to Simon Peter, and to the other disciple, whom Jesus loved, and saith unto them, They have taken away the Lord out of the sepulchre, and we know not where they have laid him.

"So they ran both together: and the other disciple did outrun Peter, and came first to the sepulchre.

"And he stooping down, and looking in, saw the linen clothes lying; yet went he not in.

"Then the disciples went away again unto their own home.

"But Mary stood without at the sepulchre weeping: and as she wept, she stooped down, and looked into the sepulchre."

*St. Matthew, xxvii:61.
†St. John, xx:1. 2. 4. 5. 10. 11.

Within it she saw two angels in white, and they asked her why she was weeping. Her reply was that they had taken away her Lord and she knew not where they had laid him. Then turning she saw Jesus "and knew not that it was Jesus," whereupon he spoke to her saying, "Woman, why weepest thou? whom seekest thou?" She in reply, mistaking him for the gardener, said: "Sir, if thou have borne him hence, tell me where thou hast laid him, and I will take him away." Jesus said, "Mary," and "she turned herself" and said, "Rabboni; which is to say, Master."

We read in Scripture that those who love God and keep His commandments will be given full measure, pressed down and running over: surely Mary received such measure for her self-sacrifice, fidelity and love, for she was the first to see the risen Christ.

Put Off the Lower Self This Christ idea is within the consciousness of everyone, but we are so engrossed with the things of the world, so blinded by material sense, and so eaten up with selfishness, that it is practically impossible for us to see with any degree of clearness that we are sons of God. The lower, loveless self must be "put off with its deeds" if we, like Mary, are to see the risen Christ, or, be lifted above the material sense of life into the glorious presence of Spirit.

The Praise of Love All the great teachers, singers and saints have joined in the song of the praise of love.

Emerson writes: "Love is omnipresent in nature as motive and reward. Love is our highest word and

the synonym of God." Love "is a fire that * * *
glows and enlarges until it warms and beams upon
multitudes of men and women, upon the universal
heart of all, and so lights up the whole world and all
nature with its generous flames." Love "expands the
sentiment; it makes the clown gentle, and gives the
coward heart." Love is a "rose of joy," and "round it
all the muses sing." "No man ever forgot the visita-
tions of that power to his heart and brain, which
created all things new; which was the dawn in him
of music, poetry, and art; which made the face of
nature radiant with purple light, the morning and the
night varied enchantments."

Shakespeare says:

> "Love is not love
> Which alters when it alteration finds,
> Or bends with the remover to remove:
> O, no! it is an ever-fixed mark,
> That looks on tempests and is never shaken;
> It is the star to every wandering bark,
> Whose worth's unknown although his height be taken."

Thomas à Kempis writes: "Nothing is sweeter
than love, nothing more courageous, nothing higher,
nothing wider, nothing more pleasant, nothing fuller
nor better in heaven and earth; because love is born
of God, and cannot rest but in God, above all created
things."

Theophrast Paracelsus, the great medieval alche-
mist, writes: "The power to recognize and follow the
truth cannot be conferred by academical degrees, it
comes only from God. * * * The highest power

of the intellect, if it is not illuminated by love is only a high grade of animal intellect."

Michael Fairless writes: "To have love is to work miracles."

And May Kendall writes: "There are two kinds of love; * * * the love that desires to love, and the love that desires to be loved. The first is always a debtor to the world, and the second always finds the world in debt to him. * * * In the midst of long-ing heart-hunger, and all the forms of selfishness, * * * there is one thing at peace. That is love."

There is absolute unanimity of opinion on this sub-ject of love so far as the above writers are concerned, and they are in complete agreement with the whole of the Scriptures. The love of Mary Magdalene is the love that is so beautifully defined by them. To sum-marize love from their point of view, we might say that it is divine; that it is a star, a fixed mark; that it is born of God and rests in God; that it illuminates the intellect, that it works miracles, and is always at peace.

The Operation of Love Since divine Love is Principle or Law, it might be interesting to show how it oper-ates in the consciousness of man.

Love is a Fire: It Warms The Bible tells us that love is a fire. and we shall proceed to show that since love is this divine fire it must both create and work miracles.

Through all the ages the sun has been used as a symbol for God, and when we look into the matter, we conclude that no better symbol could be found; for without the sun there would be no life throughout the solar system. The sun, in fact, is the central fire of the solar system, and from this centre pours forth a continuous stream of life-giving radiations.

St. Paul makes this very clear in his epistle to the Romans. If our enemy hungers, he says, we are to feed him; if he thirsts, we are to give him drink, for in so doing we shall "heap coals of fire on his head:" that we must not suffer ourselves to be overcome of evil, but that we must overcome evil with good.

This giving food and drink to our enemy and over-coming evil with good is truly the highest form of love, for when this divine fire is kindled in the consciousness of our enemy it sets him aglow with its radiant beams.

Love is always warm; it is the intellect when di-vorced from love that is cold, and hence the Bible refers to this feminine aspect of God as a divine fire. This fire is the "point within a circle," the central fire of Deity; it is Vesta, the Sun, Apollo.

The prophet Ezekiel speaks of a *fire being kindled in us, and in Jeremiah we read, †"Is not my word like as a fire? saith the Lord." and again, ‡"I will make my words in thy mouth fire."

An Embryonic Fire   God kindles this divine fire in the heart of every man, but in many it might be called an embryonic fire only, and might be likened to the latent heat stored in coal. In the past, owing to the ignorance of mankind, it was not known that this black hard cold substance could be made to liberate its heat; but now we all know, that when the

*Ezekiel. xx:47.
†Jeremiah. xxiii:29.
‡Jeremiah. v:14.

coals are surrounded with fire, they, in turn, give out the latent heat within them.

Often to the material senses man has a hard cold nature, but happy is he who is able to deny the evidence of his senses and to realize that he is the image and likeness of God in embryo. The divine fire can be made to burn brightly in his soul when he is surrounded with divine Love, for it is this Love that will help him to liberate his latent spirituality.

God's words are like a fire, and these words of truth burn like a red-hot iron into our human consciousness. When we employ this truth, fearlessly and with love giving expression to the word of God, it will be a fire in our mouth.

What a grand and inspiring thing it is to know that we can actually be the mouthpiece of God, and voice His glorious truth!

Love Guides This heavenly fire not only sets man aglow, it also serves as a light along the pathway of life. It is like a lighthouse to the tempest-tossed mariner on the sea of life, protecting him from the rocks and shoals upon which he might otherwise be shipwrecked.

In St. Paul's epistle to the Ephesians we read: *"Awake thou that sleepest, and arise from the dead, and Christ shall give thee light." Again in the second book of Samuel, †"The Lord will lighten my darkness." And St. John, in the twenty-first chapter of Revelation, in speaking of the Holy City, says that ‡"the glory of God did lighten it."

*Ephesians, v:14.
†II Samuel. xxii:29.
‡Revelation, xxi:23.

Love is a Consuming Fire This divine fire not only sets our hearts aglow and provides us with light, but it is much more than this; it is a consuming fire. There has been a great misunderstanding in the past with regard to God's love being a consuming fire. Thousands of people have been driven away from the churches by the preaching of the doctrine of everlasting punishment. They could not believe that God, if He is omnipresent Love, would condemn His erring children for ever to hell fire, since even an earthly parent would not be so unspeakably cruel.

Here we have another instance of how dangerous it is to take the Bible literally. In this case, however, the passage has been misunderstood only because mistranslated. When read in English it is most misleading.

The Word "Everlasting" For example in St. Matthew we have the following passage:

*"Wherefore if thy hand or thy foot offend thee, cut them off, and cast them from thee: it is better for thee to enter into life halt or maimed, rather than having two hands or two feet to be cast into everlasting fire."

Again in St. Matthew's gospel we read:

†"And these (that is the wicked) shall go away into everlasting punishment: but the righteous into life eternal."

And there are a number of passages in the New Testament of a similar nature.

The word translated everlasting is, however, in the

*St. Matthew, xviii :8.
†St. Matthew, xxv :46.

original Greek, αἰώνιος, and means **age-lasting**. We thus conclude that the most wicked of men are only to suffer for an age, period or cycle until such time as the error in their consciousness is burnt away or destroyed.

Some passages in the Bible where the word **everlasting** is used are correctly translated. For example, in Isaiah we find the expression, *"The everlasting Father." Now, the word used here is a Hebrew word having the sense of **continuity**; in other words, God is continually, or without interruption, the Father.

Hell Fire　Let us consider for a moment the word
Explained　hell. It is found in several passages: two occur in St. Matthew's Gospel.

†"Ye serpents, ye generation of vipers, how can ye escape the damnation of hell?"

‡"Whosoever shall say, Thou fool, shall be in danger of hell fire."

This word **hell**, as all students of the Bible know, is not hell, but the **Valley of Hinnom** or **Gehenna**, the Greek being γέεννα.

All those who have been to Jerusalem know that the Valley of Hinnom is just outside the walls of that city; and tradition says that it was in this valley the refuse from the city was burnt.

The **Valley of Hinnom**, therefore, used as an allegorical expression, represents that low state of consciousness in which the refuse or evil of our nature is burnt away. And the fire that burns it, is the fire of love. The length of time required for the destruction

*Isaiah, ix:6.
†St. Matthew, xxiii:33.
‡St. Matthew, v:22.

of this sin and error depends not only upon the measure to be consumed, but also on the tenacity with which the error is held.

· Hell then is not a place but a state of consciousness; it is within us just as the kingdom of heaven is within us. Man need not wait for death to find hell: he can discover it in this life and now.

The Call of Love   It is, however, an inspiring and comforting thought that it is always God's will to lift a man out of hell into heaven. It is always His will that man should eat of the good things from His table. The difficulty is that man, owing to his ignorance, turns from this bounteous repast. It is pathetic to read the words of Jesus:

> *"O Jerusalem, Jerusalem, thou that killest the prophets, and stonest them which are sent unto thee, how often would I have gathered thy children together, even as a hen gathereth her chickens under her wings, and ye would not!"

Love is continually calling to man to come out of the slough of despond, and climb to divine heights, where the burden will fall from his back as it fell from the back of Christian. We are all labouring under the burden of sin, but divine Love is waiting to lift this burden for us, for we read that God's yoke is easy, and His burden light. All our suffering is the direct result of our ignorance, coupled with the breaking of the divine law. Just as soon as the sin is forsaken will it be forgiven. And the fire that burns our error and sin away is Love.

*St. Matthew, xxiii:37.

Love is   Love is constructive, for while it destroys
Constructive   all that is hideous and evil, it attracts
everything that is beautiful and good.

*"And I, if I be lifted up from the earth, will
draw all men unto me."

These words of the Christ plainly show that he
must eventually draw all men away from the lower to
the higher sense of love. His love is like a magnet.

This love of God will enable us to build a beautiful
structure in our consciousness, a veritable temple of
God. It is also constructive so far as our physical
bodies are concerned, for we all know that those with
beautiful thoughts have a beautiful expression. A
beautiful mind constructs and moulds the body, and
the result is health. It is discord or ignorance, the opposite of love, which is destructive,
since it has no principle. Any man who lives a life
from which he has tried to eliminate divine Love will
find that a structure built on such a poor foundation
will come to naught. The man who thus lives is as
foolish as an architect who erects an immense building,
drawing no plans previous to the erection, and following none of the principles of architecture. This building is only erected to fall shortly into a heap of
ruins.

Luck a   The man who makes love the law of his
Misnomer   life is, to use a common expression, lucky.
And the prosperity that attends his undertakings ap-
pears to be luck.

But in God's kingdom there is no such thing as

*St. John. xii:32.

luck. Since God is Law, God can be no more accused
of a lawless act than light can be accused of producing
darkness. It is time that Christians should cease to
believe that it is impossible to be pure, loving and
good, and at the same time successful in business.
This mistake is the greatest that any one ever made.
The man whose thoughts are full of love attracts to
himself, in his business as well as in his home life,
everything that is good. He must, however, be absolutely convinced that love is omnipotent; he must
face evil fearlessly as David did Goliath. Nothing is
so insipid and unsatisfactory as the professing Christian who is lukewarm in religious matters

"Love Never *"Love never loses sight of loveliness."
Loses Sight This is true since love is itself the very
of Loveliness" essence of beauty or loveliness, and the
man who reflects this divine Love has the God-given
faculty of discovering beauty and goodness even in
those who are outwardly in the depths of degradation
and sin. Jesus possessed this power to perfection.
He was able not only to see the potential beauty in
those around him; he was able to throw so strong a
light of love upon it as to draw it from their consciousness, just as light causes the petals of a rose to unfold.

It is because "love never loses sight of loveliness,"
that in the words of Emerson already quoted, it is "the
dawn in man of music, poetry and art."

Love is Music Love is truly heavenly music, for it
awakens in man that soul-song which makes his whole
life one perfect melody. Love makes him harmonious.
The very aura or emanation of a truly loving character

*Science and Health, by Mary Baker Eddy, p. 248.

is life-giving and soothing. We are all affected by love and hate; and whereas hate is like a whirlwind which stirs up the very devil in us, love soothes and harmonizes, bringing a sense of peace, calm, rest and joy. If love never loses sight of beauty, hate never for one moment catches a glimpse of it. For to hate is to be in hell, while to love is to dwell in heaven where beauty dwells.

Love is Poetry Love more than anything else brings out the poetry in life, and it is possible to bring poetry into everything that we do. There is the poetry of motion, for the very gait of a man is changed when he becomes inspired with divine Love. His actions also cease to be prosaic, and become poetic.

Love is Art It is the aim of the artist never to lose sight of beauty. And art can be brought into the affairs of our daily life, for right living is an art, and as we try to follow out Christ's precepts, we become spiritual artists. Beauty within the consciousness creates a desire to be surrounded by all that is beautiful. Some wealthy people have articles of almost priceless value in their possession, and yet their environment is neither beautiful nor harmonious. For it is possible to gain the whole world and yet to be ignorant of the poetry and art of life. Others again, though possessed of little wealth, yet succeed in surrounding themselves with beauty. We must cultivate beauty in our minds if we would see it in the world around us, for beauty is fundamentally in mind. Colour, as a part of beauty, is a mental quality. The observant will notice that people with crude minds often wear crude colours, and that as their thought becomes more refined, the shades that formerly appealed to them cease to attract them.

Truly love is the dawn in us of music, poetry and art, since one of the attributes of love is beauty.

Love Creates Love is God, and God creates; therefore Love is the Creator, and man in God's image and likeness is also the creator of his own destiny.

Astrologers tell us that the wise man rules his stars, while the fool is ruled by them: and so the man who reflects divine Love literally rules his stars and rises above the so-called law of fate. But to make this point quite clear, we must understand what is meant by the word create. To create is to manifest God's ideas, to evolve or unfold that which is within.

There could be no growth without light and heat. It is the warmth of the sun's rays falling on the buds in springtime that causes them to unfold. To explain the unfolding of the soul of man we might use as an illustration a mother bird sitting on her eggs. She imparts warmth to the eggs, and this warmth tends to evolve the life within them. So, if we surround with love those that are dear to us, yes, and those who hate us, we shall find that their souls, too, will unfold with the fire of love, just as surely as the buds burst forth in springtime, and the birds break their shells to come out of darkness and limitation into light and freedom. We must never forget that the beautiful, the spiritual and the good are within every man, and that love causes these qualities to be made manifest. Nothing can withstand omnipotent divine Love.

A friend of mine who has been for many years a

prison missionary, and has spent his life in the endeavor to reform criminals, once told me that when in dealing with men who did not seem to possess one spark of goodness, he approached them in love—perhaps referring to the love their mothers had for them—he found instead of a hard cold nature, a nature warm and sensitive beneath the animal shell. He said they frequently broke down and wept like children. It was the love reflected by the missionary that evolved or brought into manifestation the real spiritual man hidden beneath this crust of ignorance, this mirage. For the missionary saw this outer shell as a mirage. He knew that, in spite of appearances, it was unreal.

Love Unites Again, love is the fulfilling of the law in that it brings us into unity with all that we love.

This is a great mystery, but nothing is truer or more important than this power of love. We all know how two friends who dearly love each other are at one on many points; they have much in common, they see the beauty in each other, and their hearts and lives are in tune. This attunement is sympathetic vibration. If man wishes to be in tune with infinite Love, he must let his thoughts be of such a nature that they will vibrate in sympathy with God's thoughts. Fear, worry, hate, envy, malice and revenge all have a lower rate of vibration. God is Life, Truth and Love; and when man realizes to the full that he is in the image and likeness of this Triune God, and reflects in all his thoughts, words and actions that which is harmonious, beautiful and good, he will constantly vibrate in sympathy with the great heart of God, and will hear and express divine music. To be at one with God is to grow daily in grace. To be at one with God means that the inner spiritual self grows stronger and stronger and more and more beautiful, till at last it opens into the light and presence of the Sun of Righteousness.

No one can doubt that love is the fulfilling of the law; it is the light that lighteth every man into the world; it is his star, his compass, his chart and his pilot; it will guide him across the tempestuous sea of life to that haven where all is peace and joy.

The Reign of Love   This love is truly the woman whose seed bruises the serpent's head.

*"Hers is the light of the heavens, and the brightest of the planets of the holy seven.

"She is the fourth dimension; the eyes which enlighten; the power that draweth inward to God.

"And her kingdom cometh; the day of the exaltation of woman.

"And her reign shall be greater than the reign of man: for Adam shall be put down from his place; and she shall have dominion for ever."

The "Woman Clothed with the Sun"   This Adam who is to be put down is the human, animal will-power, and in its place is to rise that spiritual, intuitive sense that cometh from within, and is the voice of God in man. This woman is none other than that mentioned in the twelfth chapter of Revelation.

> †"And there appeared a great wonder in heaven; a woman clothed with the sun, and the moon under her feet, and upon her head a crown of twelve stars."

*Clothed with the Sun, by Dr. Anna Kingsford, p. 9.
†Revelation, xii :1.

This woman clothed with the sun is really man, that is to say, man in the image and likeness of the Father-Mother-God. He is clothed with the sun inasmuch as he is surrounded with divine Light. There are many passages in the Bible which speak of the righteous shining as the sun. We read that in God there *"is no darkness at all;" so when man reflects divine Love and the woman reigns supreme in his consciousness, he literally is clothed in light.

Twelve Stars Over the woman's head are twelve stars.

These stars, from an astronomical point of view, are suns, and hence symbolize God. Their position represents intelligence. The meaning of the number twelve is significant. We are told that it symbolizes "the creature interpenetrated, as it were, by the Creator." When man reaches this state of development, his whole consciousness is interpenetrated, flooded with the light of divine Love. For just as in God there "is no darkness at all," so in man there can be no darkness when he realizes that he is in the image and likeness of his Maker.

The Moon The moon is under the woman's feet.

This indicates that she was †"victor over materiality and firm in the faith of a full intuition,—states denoted respectively by the dark and light protions of the moon; and superior evermore to the changes and chances of mortal destiny." We know that so far as the earth is concerned, only one side of the moon is seen; and furthermore, that only for a short time during the month is the moon full, and that for part of

---

*I John. 1:5.
†The Perfect Way, by Anna Kingsford, M.D., p. 188.

the time is it invisible. The moon, therefore, is a perfect symbol of the belief in dualism, that is, the belief in two powers: the one good, the other evil. Now this belief in dualism dies as soon as our consciousness is interpenetrated with light, for there are no longer dark and light portions in it, as heretofore, neither is it subject any longer to change.

The Destruction of the Red Dragon   The war in heaven spoken of in the book of Revelation is now over; the great red dragon is destroyed and he can no longer send forth his flood of error. The woman is *"at once the principle of the universe and the secret of the Intuition. She it is, the Divine woman of man's mental system, that opens to him the 'perfect way,' the 'way of the Lord,' that 'path of the just which, as a shining light, shineth more and more unto the perfect day.' And her complete restoration, crowning, and exaltation, is the one condition essential to that realization of the ideal perfection of man's nature, which, mystically, is called the 'Finding of Christ.' "

The "Woman" a Perfect Symbol   What a glorious and perfect symbol this woman is, and how we should all long and pray for the coming of that day when love shall rule supreme in our consciousness! This day will come for all. †"We know that, when he shall appear, we shall be like him; for we shall see him as he is." Even now we are the sons of God, and in due course we shall grow into a knowledge of this truth, and with faith, patience, good works and love shall eventually rise above the clouds of sin and error into the perpetual light of God.

*The Perfect Way, by Anna Kingsford. M.D., p. 6.
†I John. iii:2.

CHAPTER III.

SEVEN ASPECTS OF MAN

Self-Knowledge the Quintessence of Wisdom In Greece there were seven wise men, and these men gave utterance to seven wise sayings. The greatest of these sayings—reputed to have been made by Solon, who lived about 600 B. C.—was: "Know Thyself."

Alexander Pope must have been inspired by it when he wrote his famous lines:

"Know then thyself, presume not God to scan;
The proper study of mankind is man."

Pope looked upon the study of God as presumption, but undoubtedly the quintessence of wisdom is to know oneself since to know oneself necessarily implies a knowledge of God.

Man is Spiritual, Perfect and Sevenfold In the first chapter of Genesis we read that God created man in His own image, and gave him dominion over the fish of the sea, over the fowl of the air, and over every living thing that moved upon the earth. Truly this man is immortal, individual man with his spiritual birthright. Man is a microcosm; he is *"a centre of consciousness in the Universal Essence," or Substance, whereas generic man is God's universal idea, or the manifested spiritual universe—the macrocosm.

*Mrs. Annie Besant.

This man is not only spiritual, but perfect. Several times in the first chapter of Genesis the passage occurs, "God saw that it was good." When the creation was crowned by spiritual man, the man who knows no evil.

*"God saw everything that he had made, and, behold, it was **very good.**

†"And on the seventh day God ended his work which he had made; and he rested on the seventh day."

Now, everywhere upon this planet the number seven is in evidence, according with these seven days of creation; and man himself has a sevenfold nature. But it is not only in the aspect of possessing a sevenfold nature that man may be considered. Besides this, he is essentially one, he is dual, he is a trinity, he is fourfold, fivefold, and sixfold.

In this study of man we shall now try to explain something of his nature as seen from these different points of view.

To take man first of all as one.

Man a Microcosm   The symbol of a point within a circle is one of the oldest symbols for God. It represents the centre and circumference of being, Wisdom, Life and Love, without beginning and without end. This point within the circle is the universal Soul ,the divine Mind; and man as the microcosm is a reflection or manifestation of this infinite Mind. He, in reality, ‡"is the compound idea of God, including all right ideas." This is the higher self, the individual soul, in contradistinction to the universal Soul; and

*Genesis, 1:31.
†Genesis, ii:2.
‡Science and Health, by Mary Baker Eddy. p. 475.

to know this real inner spiritual man is the work of eternity.

We have mentioned that this point within a circle was a symbol for God, and also for man in God's image. It is interesting to note that the point within the circle is found in the lowest and minutest forms of life—in the tiny cells of which man's body and the lowest forms of vegetable life are composed, and which can be seen only through the microscope. These cells are globular or spheroidal in shape, with a central portion called the nucleus.

Now, man as the microcosm is clothed on this plane with a body composed of millions of tiny circular cells. The blood, for example, contains almost countless millions of these living creatures, called corpuscles. Wherever we look in this physical world from the highest form of life to the lowest, from man to monad, we cannot escape the point within the circle. The universe is one grand harmonious unity, and man is the image and likeness of the one Mind, one Substance, one Principle, one universal Soul, one Life, one Truth, and one Father of all.

If the work of the Creator was good, yea, very good, then its Creator must be good also. If there were any evil in the Creator, then this evil would have been made manifest in His creation.

We see then that man made in the image of God is good without admixture of evil, and that he is one in essence, since God is one.

The Dual Aspect of Man   Before discussing the dual aspect of man, it should be pointed out that the numbers used in the Bible frequently have a double meaning. There is a double meaning in this number two as applied to man. Perfect man is dual in that he is both masculine and feminine, the two natures forming a perfect whole, so that he is an expression, reflection or manifestation of the Father-Mother-God. Man is also dual in that while he is spiritual man made in the image and likeness of God the All-Wise and All-Loving, he is also mortal man, ignorant and sinning.

Let us now consider the dual nature of man in its first meaning.

Man Both Masculine and Feminine God, the great First Cause, though in His higher aspect, one, is also, as we have seen, two; for He is the Father-Mother-God. In a similar way the masculine and feminine elements are omnipresent in nature and in man. No creature has ever yet been produced except by the union of two cells, the masculine and the feminine. The origin of man's physical body can be traced to two single cells, the ovum and the spermatazoön, and it is the uniting of these two cells that brings about the body or vehicle through which man functions on this plane or in this state of consciousness. As God is Father-Mother, so man, the image and likeness of God is both masculine and feminine, neither male nor female, so perfectly and harmoniously balanced that the two principles are one. This is the real, perfect man, and it was of him that Jesus spoke when he said: "In heaven they neither marry nor are given in marriage." This heaven, of course, is the kingdom of heaven within the consciousness or soul of man. These two elements, the masculine and the feminine, are really the interblending of wisdom and love; the man representing wisdom, and the woman love.

The following extract from an ancient Indian book is of interest at this point.

"Two Halves of Gold and Silver" *"The sun is described as Brahma;—its description. Verily at first all this was non-existent; that non- existence became existent; it developed,—it became an egg: it remained [quiet] for a period of one year; it burst into two; thence were formed two halves of gold and silver."

The Dual Aspect of the Physical Body Even in man's physical body we find this dual aspect. The brain is composed of two lobes, he has two eyes, two ears, two nasal passages, two lungs, two hands and two feet. He also possesses two nervous systems, the cerebro-spinal and the sympathetic. The first might be called the masculine system, or the vehicle through which thought is expressed; while the second is the feminine system, or the instrument through which the emotions and feelings are made manifest.

There is but one heart, however; and the heart, from the physiological standpoint is the centre of life, its function being to pump the blood, which is the very essence of life, into every part of the organism; therefore we have unity as well as duality expressed in the physical body.

Spiritual and Mortal Man Now we come to the dual nature of man in its second meaning, which is diametrically opposed to its first. Looked at from this point of view, we have good and evil; light and darkness;

*Chha'ndogya Upanishad. p. 543.

man in the image and likeness of God, and ignorant, sinning, mortal man.

A Seemingly Contradictory Statement After God had finished His creation and pronounced it very good we read in the second chapter of Genesis, that *"there went up a mist from the earth, and watered the whole face of the ground." And again, "†"the Lord God formed man of the dust of the ground, and breathed into his nostrils the breath of life; and man became a living soul." Here we have a seemingly contracdictory statement, a second account, as it were of the creation of man; and the narrative goes on to state, that man partook of "the tree of knowledge of good and evil," falling from the estate wherein he was created, and that this act, or sin, was followed by suffering, disease and death.

This allegory has been a mystery to many, and the majority of the critics conclude that since the accounts contradict one another, one of them must be false.

An Analogy. The Architect, the Building and the Savage An analogy might help us at this juncture. Let us liken God to an architect—He is the great architect of the universe—and let us imagine that this architect proposes to erect a ten-story building.

Now, if this architect were to lay a foundation suitable for a two-story building, and then attempt to rear upon it a ten-story building, he would soon see his ten-story structure in a state of collapse. Therefore, before the foundations are laid, he draws the plans and completes the building in mind. Then, the concept

*Genesis, ii:6.
†Genesis, ii:7.

perfect, he is able to bring the building into manifestation, stone by stone, and brick by brick.

Let us imagine again, that while the building is still unfinished, an ignorant savage, who has never seen a building in course of construction, arrives upon the scene. He looks at the half-finished building, he sees ungainly scaffolding surrounding it, dirty navvies hurrying about, piles of bricks and heaps of mortar lying on every side; everything to his untutored eye is in disorder and confusion; in short, he sees only evil.

Standing by the savage is the architect. Nothing could be more dissimilar than the impression made upon his mind, and the impression made upon the mind of the savage.

The architect sees the bricks and mortar lying about, but he knows that they all have their place, and will eventually become part of the structure. The navvies he also recognizes as helpers, the scaffolding as transitory, and as set up solely to aid in the erection of the building. The savage gazes at the scene with ignorant eyes: the architect sees it through the eyes of intelligence. So where the savage sees nothing but chaos, the architect sees order and arrangement; he knows that the building, at present limited to one story, will be less limited later; that as time goes on, story after story will be added until finally his idea has been brought into complete manifestation.

And now let us use the analogy to illustrate our subject.

God's Idea Gradually Unfolded Perfect man, like the plans of the building, exists as a perfect idea in the mind of God, and this idea is gradually being unfolded or brought into manifestation.

At first, we may say, Adam, the man created out of the dust of the ground, consists, like the building, of but one story; he is not yet the complete expression of God's perfect idea; he is not man in the absolute sense: he is relative man, he is man in a state of limitation. This state of limitation is evil, and in this state man makes many mistakes and breaks the laws of God. Yet this limitation or evil is negation: it is not really a power opposed to God, but a want of understanding on the part of Adam. As Adam unfolds, or as this beautiful structure of truth and love is gradually brought into manifestation, the evil falls away, just as the scaffolding is taken down as soon as the ten-story building is completed. In this way, man has two natures.

The First and Last Man Adam It might interest the reader at this point to note what St. Paul has to say upon this subject. Several passages in the first epistle to the Corinthians help us to its right understanding.

*"For as in Adam all die, even so in Christ shall all be made alive.

.   .   .   .

"For he must reign, till he hath put all enemies under his feet.

"The last enemy that shall be destroyed is death.

.   .   .   .

"There are also celestial bodies, and bodies terrestrial: but the glory of the celestial is one, and the glory of the terrestrial is another.

.   .   .   .

*I Corinthians, xv:22, 25, 26, 40, 42-45, 47, 50, 53.

"So also is the resurrection of the dead. It is sown in corruption; it is raised in incorruption:

"It is sown in dishonour; it is raised in glory: it is sown in weakness; it is raised in power:

"It is sown a natural body; it is raised a spiritual body. There is a natural body, and there is a spiritual body.

"And so it is written, The first man Adam was made a living soul; the last Adam was made a quickening spirit.

.   .   .   .

"The first man is of the earth, earthy: the second man is the Lord from heaven.

.   .   .   .

"*   *   * Flesh and blood cannot inherit the kingdom of God; neither doth corruption inherit incorruption.

.   .   .   .

"For this corruptible must put on incorruption, and this mortal must put on immortality."

The Temporal and Eternal St. Paul goes on to tell us that the sting of death is sin, but that we gain the victory through Christ. He also says:

*"Our light affliction, which is but for a moment, worketh for us a far more exceeding and eternal weight of glory;

"While we look not at the things that are seen, but at the things which are not seen:" (i.e. seen with the physical eyes) "for the things

*II Corinthians, iv:17, 18.

which are seen are temporal; but the things which are not seen are eternal."

Here we have the two natures or aspects of man perfectly described. St. Paul makes it clear that this outer animal man which is seen, is like the scaffolding of the building: it is temporal and therefore technically unreal; the affliction is but for a moment, and will quickly pass away when the inner spiritual man is unfolded.

Job's Description of Mortal Man   In the book of Job we find a vivid word picture of mortal man. He possesses *"months of vanity, and wearisome nights are appointed" unto him. His "days are swifter than a weaver's shuttle, and are spent without hope." His life is wind: he vanishes away as a cloud.

Contrast with this picture St. Paul's magnificent description of the spiritual man which we have just read—of that celestial, glorious and incorruptible being, the inner and unseen image of God, the conqueror of his enemies, the destroyer of death. This man is as different from the old man Adam as the scaffolding is different from the beautiful structure within it.

The Transmutation of the Lower Nature   To know ourselves rightly, we must learn to recognize these two natures, and we must realize that the lower nature is not to be ignored, any more than the scaffolding is to be ignored: it has its present usefulness. But this lower self, or old man, is to be educated out of itself until it no longer exists. This is transmutation

*Job, vii:1-10.

or transformation. By the renewing of the mind we prove *"what is that good, and acceptable, and perfect, will of God."

Adam Defined The Hebrew for Adam is Adm, which literally means "of the ground." These three letters indicate that man is first A. or Adam; later he develops into D. or David, whose son is the Christ or Messiah, or M. This man of the dust of the ground is St. Paul's old man who is to be put off with his deeds.

Eve Taken from Adam's Side This Adam, the red man, gives birth to his higher self, the woman; and this woman is taken from his side. When a grain of corn is planted in the ground it bursts open, and out of its side comes a little sprout. This grows and grows until eventually it develops into a head of wheat. In like manner Eve is taken from Adam's side, when a deep sleep falls upon him,—a sleep which might be compared to the dying of the grain in the earth.

The Meaning of Eve The meaning of Heva, the Sanscrit for Eve, is "that which completes life." Eve thus completes Adam's life. Eve is, in one of her aspects, love: so also is the seed produced by her, and it is because that seed is love that it is able to bruise the serpent's head.

Man's Triune Nature Let us next consider the threefold nature of man.

In St. Paul's first epistle to the Thessalonians we find this passage:

*Romans. xii:2

*"And the very God of peace sanctify you wholly; and I pray God your whole **spirit and soul and body** be preserved blameless unto the coming of our Lord Jesus Christ."

Here we see that man is spoken of as a being composed of spirit and soul and body. If God is three—and all the religions through all the ages have represented Him as a trinity in unity—then man in God's image must also have a triune nature. The number three or the triangle is frequently used to represent man's higher nature in contradistinction to the number four which symbolizes his lower nature. But this number four will be explained more fully later.

In Plato's "Timaeus," according to W. Wynn Westcott, we have the Divine Triad, namely: †"Theos—God, Logos—the Word, and Psyche—the Soul." The Brahmins, he also says, speak of "the three fires," as "being the three aspects of the human soul," namely: "Atma, Buddhi, Manas."

The Sacred Number Three and the Tabernacle This sacred number three is found everywhere in the Bible.

The Tabernacle was fashioned on the number three.

‡The chief parts were the Holy of Holies, the Holy Place, and the Court. In the Holy of Holies there were three pieces of furniture, the ark and the mercy seat and the cherubim; in the Holy Place, the altar of incense and the candlestick and the table of shewbread; and in the Court, the altar and the laver and its foot.

*I Thessalonians, v:23.
†Numbers, by W. Wynn Westcott, pp. 43, 47.
‡Exodus, xxv-xxvii, xxxv-xxxviii. Chapters on Symbolism, by W. Frank Shaw, p. 60.

There were also three veils, one before each of the main parts of the building. Three colours were used: blue, purple and scarlet. There were three pillars on each side of the entrance to the Court. In examining the candlestick we notice that there were three branches and three bowls on either side. And the Israelites made offerings in gold and silver and brass.

Now the Tabernacle is an allegory of man.

A full explanation of the significance of its different parts would be out of place here, since we are dealing with only the number three; but the symbolism of one or two of its features might be pointed out.

The Holy of Holies   The Holy of Holies represents man's inner, spiritual nature, where God speaks to him, *"the secret place of the most High." and the †"closet" which Jesus on one occasion mentioned.

The Holy Place   The Holy Place was midway between the Holy of Holies and the Court. The Holy Place therefore would represent the soul.

The Court   The Court would symbolize the body.

With regard to the employment of the materials gold, silver and brass, we find that gold, the purest of metals, was used in the Holy of Holies and in the Holy Place as symbolizing the purity of the divine Mind and of man's higher self. The ark, the mercy seat, the cherubim, the table of shewbread, the vessels upon it, the altar of incense, the candlestick, and the pillars upon which the vail was hung that divided the sanctuary from the Court: all these were either of pure gold, or were overlaid with gold.

*Psalms. xci:1.
†St. Matthew, vi:6

Silver, being less precious, was used in the Court for the making of the hooks and the fillets for the pillars, and for the overlaying of the chapiters; and was found elsewhere in the Tabernacle only in the making of "the sockets of the sanctuary and the sockets of the vail."

Brass, which represents man's outer, sense nature—that portion which is to be sacrificed or transmuted into pure gold—was used in the Court where the sacrifices were made. The altar of burnt offering was overlaid with it. The utensils used at the altar, the laver and its foot, the sockets of the Court, the pins of the Tabernacle and of the Court were all of brass. The reader might also be reminded that Goliath's armour was made of brass.

King Solomon's Temple   We find the figure three also in evidence when we turn to the account of the building of King Solomon's Temple. There we read that *the height was three score cubits, that the inner court was built of three rows of hewed stone, and that there were three chambers built against the wall: a nethermost, a middle, and a third chamber, connected by winding stairs.

The Temple, as well as the Tabernacle, is a symbol of man.

Jesus in speaking of it made the significant remark that if it were destroyed, he would build it again in three days. †"But he spake of the temple of his body."

But it might be asked why the Tabernacle and the Temple are employed as symbols of man.

*I Kings. vi.
†St. John, 11:21.

Christ Officiates in the Temple St. Paul makes this point clear when he tells us that we are to be priests unto God. Now Christ Jesus is frequently spoken of as the great High Priest, and Christ, we are told, is in us. If man is the temple, and Christ is in him, then it is this Christ in man who is to officiate in the temple. Christ is "the Son"—the "Christ-Principle as represented in the Trinity—the result of one and two." Again, Christ is *"the divine manifestation of God, which comes to the flesh to destroy incarnate error."

From the above definitions it is plainly seen that from a symbolical point of view no better number than three could be employed. It is in fact the perfect number—the three in one, the one in three.

The Fourfold Nature of Man We will now consider man as possessing a fourfold nature.

Just as three symbolizes man's higher self, so four symbolizes his lower self and the physical body. This number is sometimes spoken of as the "square of matter."

The following are a few of the instances in which the number four is regarded in this light:

The "Square of Matter" The earth, according to the account of the creation in the first chapter of Genesis, was formed on the fourth day. Jerusalem in which Solomon's Temple was built is spoken of as a four-sided city. The altar was four-square, with a ring of gold at each of its four corners.

Isaac Myer declares that man displays "four evil

*Science and Health, by Mary Baker Eddy, p. 583.

tendencies, * * * an evil inclination, evil thoughts, evil words and evil actions;" and according to W. Frank Shaw, "four symbolizes the world," because it "arises immediately" out of three, the trinity.

The Tabernacle Fourfold In the following extract we observe how the Tabernacle is not only threefold but fourfold:

*"The idea of this heavenly Salem is expressed also in the Tabernacle of Moses. For this, too, was fourfold. The Outer Court, which was open, denoted the Body or Man physical and visible; the covered Tent, or Holy place, denoted the Man intellectual and invisible; and the Holy of Holies within the veil, denoted the Heart or Soul, itself the shrine of the Spirit of the man, and of the divine Glory, which, in their turn, were typified by the Ark and Shekinah. And in each of the four Depositaries were three utensils illustrative of the regenerative degrees belonging to each division."

This number four is to be eventually redeemed or transformed, so we must not look upon it as wholly evil, but rather as a limited or transitory state of things.

Everything in Reality is Spiritual If God created the world, and God is Spirit, then everything in reality is spiritual and not material, so that the true and higher aspect of this number symbolizes good; indeed, all is good. If we mortals could only remove the veil from before our eyes which prevents us from seeing things as they really are, we should see that matter (symbolized by four) is really a manifestation of God.

*The Perfect Way, by Anna Kingsford M. D., pp. 243, 244.

The Ark, for example, had four rings of gold cast for its four corners, by which it was to be carried, and it is reocrded that *"In the fourth year was the foundation of the house of the Lord laid." It is also interesting to note that $1+2+3+4=10=1$. ($10=1$ because $1+0=1$).

The Four Causes of Aristotle

We might here enumerate the four Causes of Aristotle, mentioned by W. Wynn Westcott in his book on "Numbers."

"Divinity as the cause   —by which;
Matter   —from which;
Form   —through which;
Effect with reference to which."

Spirit is Cause; the Universe is Effect

It would be less misleading if we substitute for the word matter the words manifestation of Spirit, since Spirit is Cause and the universe is effect. Therefore the number four has a place in the divine scheme, and it is our duty to find its place. Seven primary colours are necessary in the production of white, and the number four is equally necessary in the evolution of man.

Man's Fivefold Aspect

We will now leave the square, and turn to the fivefold aspect of man.

Its symbolic figure is a five-pointed star. It has been said that five †"represents man in opposition to matter. Five is dual in nature and will bring

"Man in Opposition to Matter"

joy and crucifixion, just according to the way in which it is used—whether used with understanding or otherwise. It is

*I Kings. vi :37.
†Zillah Jelliman.

nature's number and is represented by the pentagram which shows the figure of a man, with the head in the spiritual, arms outstretched east and west, and feet on earth."

Five Defined   W. Frank Shaw defines five as *"the number of expiation, and of sacrifice."

In **The Perfect Way** we read:

The Five Senses   †"And the crucified, regenerate Man, having made At-one-ment throughout his own fourfold nature, and with the Father through Christ, bears about in himself the 'marks' of the Lord, —the five wounds of the five senses evercome, the 'stigmata' of the Saints."

Man has a limited, material sense of life. He is, however, to be educated, not condemned: he is to be taught the truth. Material sense must be transmuted into spiritual perception, and as the transmutation proceeds, he gains a higher and more exalted sense of things.

The following passage from one of the Upanishads throws some light on this number as typical of man:

‡"Him we consider as a river, whose water is derived from five currents (the five senses of intellect), which is fearful and crooked, by its five sources, (the five elements), whose waves are the five (vital) airs, whose origin is the producer of the five senses of intellect (the mind), which has five whirlpools, (the objects of the senses), which is impelled by the velocity of the five kinds of pain, which is divided by the five kinds of misery, and which has five turnings."

*Chapters on Symbolism. by W. Frank Shaw. p. 77.
†The Perfect Way. by Anna Kingsford M. D.. p. 107.
‡S'we'ta's'watara Upanishad. p. 381.

The Curtains of the Tabernacle In studying the construction of the Tabernacle, we find that two different kinds of curtains were to be employed.

The first kind was to be made "of fine twined linen, and blue, and purple, and scarlet," and was to be in two sets of five and five.

*"The five curtains shall be coupled together one to another; and other five curtains shall be coupled one to another."

And they were to be coupled together with fifty taches of gold, so that the Tabernacle should be one.

The second kind was to be made of goat's hair, and was to be used as a covering upon the Tabernacle, and was to be in two sets of five and six.

†"And thou shalt couple five curtains by themselves, and six curtains by themselves."

These were to be coupled together by taches of brass.

We should notice the numbers and metals associated with these two kinds of curtains. The first two sets when added together produce ten, which, in its highest significance or aspect, symbolizes divine Principle or Law. Therefore these curtains, as is fit, were fastened with gold.

The Goat The second kind of curtains were made of goat's hair. Now the goat was a symbol of evil, (the lower animal physical nature, which is to be put off, sacrificed, burned, destroyed, transformed or transmuted) as we may see by reference to the parable of the

*Exodus, xxvi:3.
†Exodus, xxvi:9.

*Last Judgment, and the ceremony of atonement in which the †scapegoat, bearing the sins of the people was driven out into the wilderness. Also, the two **The Number** sets added together totalled eleven, and, **Eleven** according to W. Wynn Westcott, the number eleven ‡"seems to have been the type of a number with an evil reputation among all peoples. The Kabalists contrasted it with the perfection of the Decad, and just as the Sephirotic number is the form of all good things, so eleven is the essence of all that is sinful, harmful and imperfect. * * *

"It is called the 'Number of Sins' and the 'Penitent,' because it exceeds the number of the Commandments and is less than twelve, which is the number of Grace and Perfection." Again ‖"Eleven symbolizes transgression, iniquity, and sin, because it oversteps the Law of God laid down in the Ten commandments."

Therefore it is appropriate that these curtains should be fastened with brass instead of gold.

The But the most significant use of the num-**Measurements** ber five lies in the measurements of the **of the Altar** altar. The command was given: "Thou shalt make an altar * * * five cubits long, and five cubits broad." It will be remembered that animals were sacrificed upon the altar. Now, if "five is the number of expiation and sacrifice," we conclude that it is the animal nature that must die or be sacrificed. This sacrifice is in fact the crucifixion of the flesh, or fleshly sensual animal self.

This is the lower interpretation of the number five.

*Matthew, xxv:31-46.
†Leviticus, xvi.
‡Numbers, by W. Wynn Westcott, pp. 100, 101.
‖Chapters in Symbolism, by W. Frank Shaw, p. 106.

The Higher Interpretation of the Number Five And now for the higher. For, in knowing ourselves, it is always well to distinguish between this higher and lower interpretation.

When this crucifixion of the flesh is accomplished, man is no longer the old Adam: he is a new man in Christ Jesus.

Now we see our Pentagram, symbolic of crucifixion, shining out at last—a star of joy; for man, become divine, shines like a star or a sun: he is literally a "shining one."

We read: *"The soul that sinneth it shall die." And yet David exclaims: †"He restoreth my soul." It is evident then that as we put off the lower animal sense, through a knowledge of the Truth, we have our spiritual sense of life restored to us.

‡"And there was given me a reed like unto a rod; and the angel stood, saying, Rise, and measure the temple of God, and the altar, and them that worship therein.

"But the court which is without the temple leave out, and measure it not."

Man, Sixfold And now for the sixfold aspect of man,
Six has for its symbolic figure a double triangle, each of the triangles being equilateral and equiangular.

The Shield of David Explained One triangle has its apex pointing upward, and represents the triune God. The other has its apex pointing downward, and represents: first the universe, macrocosm or God

*Ezekiel, xviii :4.
†Psalms, xxiii :3.
‡Revelation, xi :1. 2.

made manifest; and secondly man in God's image and likeness, the microcosm—created, let us remember, on the sixth day. The two triangles when united give us the six-pointed star, *"Hexapla, or Hexalpha, the Shield of David. * * * It must not be confused with the Pentalpha which is the true Solomon's seal."

Why should this shield be called the Shield of David?

Christ, as we have already explained, is spoken of as the Son of David because he springs from David, the partly-regenerate man; and Christ in turn is the divine Idea of God made manifest in the flesh, the perfect man, God's image and likeness. In other words, the second triangle is the Triune God, or the first triangle, made manifest. These two triangles are in reality one figure. †"In Christian Churches we find the Hexalpha used to express the union of the divine and human natures, deemed to exist in Jesus the Christ of the New Testament."

When we realize that we are at one with God, as Jesus realized it when he said, ‡"I and my Father are on," when we let this great truth be our shield, then we need fear nothing, for by its power we shall be protected from all the fiery darts of error, and be enabled like David to conquer the great Goliath.

Six Defined The figure six plays a big part in symbolism.

‖"Nicomachus calls it 'the form of form, the only number adapted to the Soul, the distinct union of the parts of the universe.'"

---

*Numbers. by W. Wynn Westcott. p. 69.
†Ibid.
‡St. John, x:30.
‖Numbers. by W. Wynn Westcott. p. 64.

*"According to the Pythagoreans, after a period of 216 years, which number is the cube of 6, all things are regenerated.

†"The circumference of a globe has been fixed at 360 degrees, six sixties; the hour divided into 60 minutes, each of 60 seconds. The Tartars had a period of 60 days, the Chinese also; and the Asiatics generally a period of 60 years. The Babylonian great period was 3600 years, the Naros multiplied by 6.

The Lily   "The 'Lily' which in all the old Annunciation pictures Gabriel presents to the Virgin has 6 leaves, and the flower shows 6 petals all alike, around a central three-headed stigma, as is botanically correct. One of the three main divisions into which plants are arranged by Botanists, is typified by a predominance of the numbers 3 and 6, in all parts of the flowers, 6 leaves forming a perianth, 6 stamens, and a 3-lobed stigma with a 3- or 6-celled ovary is the common arrangement."

The fact that the numbers three and six appear so frequently in the formation of flowers, particularly in the lily, reminds us that the universe is a reflection or manifestation of Spirit.

The Inverted Let us now consider the lower or inverted
Aspect of the aspect of this number.
Number Six   ‡"Six is the number of temptation and sin; and also of toil and punishment of sin. * * *

"The whole idea of conflict and distress 'culminates in the 666, the mark of the Beast.'"

*Numbers, by W. Wynn Westcott, p. 66.
†Ibid, p. 69.
‡Chapters in Symbolism, by W. Frank Shaw, pp. 31, 34.

· Six has also been defined as the *"Number of struggle and difficulty. The number of imitation brings
obstacles, but all of these can be overcome and the
Ego can triumph through 1. 2. 3. 4. 5. 6═21═3—△—
living up to the Christ principle and keeping a perfect
triangle. Balance, poise, judgment."

It will be noticed that 21, separated into its com-
ponent parts 2 and 1, and added together, equals 3.

Bible Excerpts. Instances of the Use of the Number Six The following are a few instances of the use of the number six as symbolizing toil and suffering:

The sixth petition of the Lord's Prayer reads, "Lead us not into temptation."

The children of Israel were instructed to gather
manna during six days of the week, and this gathering
of manna denoted "toil in this world."

Our Lord, according to St. John, was sentenced to
be crucified at the sixth hour of the sixth day.

In the twelfth verse of the sixth chapter of Revelation we read: "And I beheld when he had opened
the sixth seal, and, lo, there was a great earthquake."
This earthquake symbolizes the "time of suffering to
the church," and this church it must be remembered
is the temple of truth and love in the consciousness of
each individual.

The great flood mentioned in the Old Testament
occurred in the six hundredth year of Noah's life.

In studying the symbolism of numbers, it must be
borne in mind that it is not only the original number
that is considered. The number is frequently multiplied by other numbers. The number ten is often em-

*Zillah Jelliman.

ployed. For example, the six hundred years referred to as the age of Noah is produced by multiplying six by ten, and the result sixty, by ten; or by squaring ten and then multiplying the result one hundred, by six.

The Dual Aspect of Six But it may be asked why this number six, which symbolizes sin and suffering for sin, can also represent God and His spiritual universe, including man in God's image and likeness.

This is really answered in our discussion on evil and its origin. It is owing to man's limited, materialistic sense of life or ignorance that he sins and suffers, and although the stupendous fact that man is in the image and likeness of God is perfectly true, yet at this period man is by no means fully aware of it. However, as the Christ idea grows and unfolds within his consciousness, he will rise above this sense of limitation and pain, as we have seen in the transformation of 21 into 3, the former number representing the sum of the first six numerals. This symbolism shows how step by step man climbs the ladder of life until he at last reaches reality, the divine Triad, God.

Man's Sevenfold Nature Above all things it is essential that man should comprehend that he is a divine being with the sevenfold nature.

Solomon's Temple was *seven years in building, and symbolically the temple of truth and love in our consciousness is completed in seven years.

The figure symbolic of seven is the combination of a square and a triangle. The divine Triad, the Christ, enters the square or the four-sided city of Jerusalem and transforms it into the New Jerusalem, no longer

*I Kings, vi:38.

four but seven. The Egyptians expressed this number by means of a pyramid, with its four-sided base and triangular sides with the apex pointing heavenward.

The number seven seems to run through the whole of man's life.

At seven months the young baby cuts its first tooth, and the first set of teeth are complete at the end of seven years. There is usually quite a marked change in a child at this age: it seems to express more individuality than at any other previous period of its existence. Some psychologists state that it is at seven years that the ego fully ensouls the body. Puberty or the period of adolescence is reached at fourteen years of age, or seven times two. At seven times three the physical body should be fully developed, and it is during the period of from forty-two to forty-nine that the "change of life" occurs. At forty-nine our reason is supposed to be fully matured.

Seven Heavenly Bodies and the Corresponding Minerals and Animals

*"Duncan assigns these Minerals and Animals to the 7 Heavenly Bodies known to the ancient world.

"Moon	Bull	Silver
Mercury	Serpent	Quicksilver
Venus	Dove	Copper
Sun	Lion	Gold
Mars	Wolf	Iron
Jupiter	Eagle	Pewter
Saturn	Ass	Lead."

*Numbers, by W. Wynn Westcott, p. 77.

*"An ancient symbol of the universe was a ship with seven pilots, in the centre of the ship, a lion; possibly from an idea that the Sun first rose in Leo."

Seven Defined This number seven is also defined as †"the key to the whole life of the ego." It is "another form of the one." Thus: "1. 2. 3. 4. 5. 6. 7.=28=10=1."

W. Frank Shaw describes seven as ‡"the special symbol and token of the intercourse of God with the world, of the Communion of the Creator with the creature."

Solomon's Temple Completed the Seventh Year If, as has been stated, this number seven is "the key to the whole life of the ego," we can readily understand why the Bible says that Solomon's Temple was not complete until the seventh year. Symbolically the number seven is just as essential to man as are seven notes to complete the musical scale, and seven primary colours to complete the spectrum.

Two Paths from which to Choose It is a glorious and comforting thought that this lower self symbolized by the number four eventually disappears, being transmuted or transformed into seven; and just to the extent that man allows God to rule his life, just to that extent will pain and suffering be eliminated from it. There are two paths from which to choose: the straight and narrow path of joy, and the long and tortuous path of suffering.

It might be interesting to examine more in detail both the Tabernacle made by Moses and the Temple

*Numbers, by W. Wynn Westcott, p. 78.
†Zillah Jelliman.
‡Chapters in Symbolism, by W. Frank Shaw, p. 85.

built by Solomon, in so far as they relate to man and his sevenfold nature.

Man the Temple of God

For one of the first things for man to realize is that he is literally a temple of God. *"For we know," says St. Paul, "that if our earthly house of this tabernacle were dissolved, we have a building of God, an house not made with hands, eternal in the heavens." Again, †"Know ye not that ye are the temple of God?" And again, ‡"What? know ye not that your body is the temple of the Holy Ghost which is in you, which ye have of God?"

Twofold Meaning of Temple

Like many other symbols, this tabernacle or temple has a twofold meaning. In its higher sense, man himself is the temple of God: in its lower sense man's body is that temple. There are many passages in which the word is used in this lower sense.

The Tabernacle and Temple a Study in Symbolism

All the measurements of both the Tabernacle and the Temple have a symbolic meaning, as have also the materials of which they were made.

First we notice that it was necessary for a sanctuary to be made where God might dwell among His people.

Although man lives and moves and has his being in Spirit, it is necessary, in order that he may discern the still small voice of Spirit, that a sanctuary should be built—the closet of which Jesus spoke; otherwise

*II Corinthians. v:1.
†I Corinthians. iii:16.
‡I Corinthians. vi:19.

it is impossible for him to enter it, shut his door and pray to his Father in secret.

The mercy seat was of pure gold, as also were the cherubims. The use of gold denotes that the purer we are in thought the easier it is for us to commune with God. *"Blessed are the pure in heart," said Jesus, "for they shall see God." And the promise to Moses was: †"There I will meet with thee, and I will commune with thee from above the mercy seat, from between the two cherubims which are upon the ark of the testimony, of all things which I will give thee in commandment unto the children of Israel."

There is one point of difference that might be noticed between the Tabernacle and the Temple.

The Tabernacle was a movable sanctuary: the Temple was a permanent building.

While the children of Israel were wandering in the wilderness, they were obliged to have a sanctuary that could be easily transported: when they had reached the promised land, and their wanderings and wars were over, then they could build their Temple.

Man a Nomad Man in the early stages of his spiritual development is a nomad, wandering in the wilderness of sense. His desires lead him from place to place, and having no fixed abode he dwells in a tent. His thoughts are superficial, and his mind wanders, because his ability or power to concentrate is lacking. Later, when he gains more wisdom, he builds a firm foundation of stone, upon which is erected a permanent superstructure. While in the former state of consciousness he worships God in the tabernacle, but later he

*St. Matthew, v:8.
†Exodus, xxv:22.

communes with his Father in the inner sanctuary of the temple.

We, like the Israelites, may be still wandering in the wilderness. The sanctuary of truth and love that we are building in consciousness cannot be erected in one lifetime and may be only a tabernacle. But even though the building is at first a movable one, there is no reason why we should be discouraged or feel that it is impossible for us to commune with God. We may be children in spiritual things, lacking in experience and understanding, but this does not excuse us from taking just as much care in building this first tabernacle as is exercised in the construction of the temple at a later date.

Concerning the building of Solomon's Temple we read:

Solomon's Temple Erected on a Stone Foundation   *"They brought great stones, costly stones, and hewed stones, to lay the foundation of the house.

"And Solomon's builders and Hiram's builders did hew them, and the stonesquarers: so they prepared timber and stones to build the house."

Just as Solomon was careful to lay a firm foundation, so, in building our temple, must we be. And our foundation and our chief corner stone is Christ Jesus, the Christ-idea in man.

Again we read:

No Tool of Iron was Heard   †"And the house, when it was in building, was built of stone made ready before it was brought

*I Kings. v:17, 18.
†I Kings. vi:7.

thither: so that there was neither hammer nor axe nor any tool of iron heard in the house, while it was in building."

This house is immaterial in every sense of the word, since during the building of the Temple no tool of iron was heard: the carnal mind and the human will-power have nothing to do with the building of this glorious structure.

The Winding There is symbolic interest in the winding
Stairs stairs mentioned in the eighth verse of the sixth chapter. This spiral is not only used symbolically, but is found actually in all the kingdoms of nature from the mineral up to man. Astronomers, in observing nebulæ, tell us of some that are spiral in form. It may be possible therefore that the solar system is literally and actually constructed on this basis. Our spiritual growth is very much like a spiral, for it seems at times as though we have made little headway, as though we were back again at the point from which we had set out; but though we seem to be at the same point, we are a little higher up than we were before. Every cycle lifts us nearer heaven. or reality: assured of this truth, we must keep on climbing, and never look back.

Man Makes We must also be content to make this
His Ascent ascent step by step, walking constantly in
Step by Step the footsteps of Christ our way-shower. If we grow weary we have only to look to God for strength to help us in our journey upward: the higher we ascend, the rarer and purer becomes the atmos-

phere, and the more extended the view, until at last we find ourselves above the clouds of ignorance, basking in the glorious sunshine of Truth and Love.

It is important for us to ascertain what stage we have reached in this heavenly journey, for all of us are at different stages. Some are half-way up the staircase; some have not yet reached that point; others again are many steps above it.

Never Yield to Discouragement We are not to be disheartened or discouraged if our brother seems to be making better progress than we are: we have an individuality of our own, and it is our duty to follow the line of this individuality. St. Paul sets us an inspiring example:

Do Not Look Back *"Forgetting," he says, "those things which are behind, and reaching forth unto those things which are before,

"I press toward the mark for the prize of the high calling of God in Christ Jesus."

There are many battles to be fought, and many inclinations to be sacrificed, before we reach the New Jerusalem, that four-sided heavenly city mentioned in Revelation—a city needing no light of the sun, for the glory of God is the light thereof; a city four-square, yet nevertheless a city with streets of gold, streets which are pure channels in consciousness. When we have entered into that city, then the triangle, with its purifying influence, has entered the square, and there dwells in us that mind which was also in Christ Jesus.

*Philippians. iii:13, 14.

The Holy City In examining this city we find that in each of the four sides, there are three gates: three on the east, three on the west, three on the north and three on the south. Here we have the number twelve —"the creature interpenetrated * * * by the Creator." Just as the woman was crowned by twelve stars, so this heavenly city is surrounded by twelve gates.

The Number Twelve Defined The following passage throws some light on the number twelve:·

"When the cycle of creation is complete, whether of the macrocosm or of the microcosm, the Great Work is accomplished. Six for the manifestation, and six for the interpretation: six for the outgoing, and six for the ingathering: six for the man, and six for the woman.

"Then shall be the Sabbath of the Lord God."

Twelve Pearly Gates In the New Jerusalem each gate is a pearl, and standing at each gate to guard it is an angel—a winged messenger of Truth and Love. No evil can touch the man in whose consciousness the heavenly city is established, for it is utterly impossible for evil to overcome good as for darkness to dissipate light. There is no night in that city, and the gates are never closed.

The Red Dragon Conquered How inspiring it is to know that the great red dragon is conquered and chained in the pit! as conquered and chained he is indeed, since evil is negation or ignorance. And although we seem to be making slow progress on this journey of life, wandering like the children of Israel in the wilderness, yet there is always an abundant supply of manna to be gathered day by day, and for these blessings received in the wilderness our hearts

Fix Your Eye on the Perfect Christ-Ideal must be full of gratitude. Above all we must keep our eyes fixed on the perfect Christ-idea, knowing full well that one day *"we shall be like him; for we shall see him as he is." As a sense of this truth deepens in our consciousness, we shall rejoice increasingly in the knownedge that †"the things which are seen are temporal; but the things which are not seen are eternal."

Let us do all in our power to know the truth, to remove the scales from our eyes. We must eventually know ourselves, since as God's image we reflect divine Wisdom.

Alexander Pope says that man stands at present on an "isthmus of a middle state;" that he has too much knowledge to be a sceptic and too much weakness to be a stoic; that he is "born but to die, and reasons but to err;" that in his nature there is "chaos of thought and passion, all confused."

Spiritual Man the Glory of the World But he shows us also the spiritual side of man, which is the true side. He declares that by force divine, his self-love becomes the scale to measure the wants of others by his own; that in his higher self man is "great lord of all things, sole judge of truth, and the glory * * * of the world."

Truly man has two natures: the mortal and the

*I John. iii:2.
†II Corinthians. iv:18.

divine. But the 'divine must eventually gain the ascendancy, since Spirit is all-good and all-powerful.

SUMMARY

Man the microcosm is a point within a circle; the image and likeness of God, the one Substance or Spirit; a centre of consciousness in Spirit.

He is two halves of a perfect whole; the image or reflection of the Father-Mother-God; the manifestation or expression of divine Intelligence and Love.

*He is a trinity in unity, being composed of spirit, soul and body; he is threefold, being a manifestation of the Universal Soul, the Holy Trinity.

He is fourfold, especially in his material nature, and may be represented by a quadrangle.

He is fivefold since he has five senses, and may be represented by a pentagram. When these senses have been crucified, he shines like a five-pointed star.

He is sixfold, and since he is a manifestation of the Holy Trinity, he may be represented by a double triangle or a six-pointed star.

He is sevenfold since the Christ-idea, the triangle, is within his four-sided material nature; and he may therefore be represented by a combined square and triangle forming a pyramid.

*The above is Plato's idea. Some authorities give spirit, mind and body as the triune nature of man. There are many classifications. For a full explanation see The Christian Creed, by C. W. Leadbeater, plate II., p. 37.
* The Key to Theosophy, by H. P. Blavatsky, p. 62.

CHAPTER IV.

THE WAY

The Christ Way   Jesus replying to the question of Thomas, "How can we know the way?" said: *"I am the way, the truth, and the life: no man cometh unto the Father, but by me."

This Christ Way is straight and narrow, and we are told that there are few who find it. On the broad road we meet with suffering: with sin, disease and death; along the Christ Way we have the star of truth to guide us. Christ has traversed this road before us, so we need not fear to tread in it: we have but to walk where he has led.

We will now consider the chief footsteps or milestones along this straight and narrow road.

A Knotty Problem   In the first chapter of the gospel according to St. Matthew, those who take the Scriptures literally find a knotty problem. The first sixteen verses name the generations from Abraham to †"Joseph the husband of Mary, of whom was born Jesus, who is called Christ." The narrator takes all the trouble to give these generations only to inform us in the end that Joseph was not the father of Jesus Christ, since Jesus Christ was immaculately conceived.

*St. John. xiv:5, 6.
†St. Matthew, I:16.

We are thus faced by the discovery that, since Joseph is not the father of Christ, Christ, who is repeatedly called the son of David, is not the son of David at all. Why then is this genealogy mentioned, and what is the meaning of these seemingly contradictory statements?

The problem is quite easy to solve when we interpret this chapter allegorically.

In the seventeenth verse we read: ·

The Forty-Two Generations from Abraham to Christ
"So all the generations from Abraham to David are fourteen generations; and from David until the carrying away into Babylon are fourteen generations; and from the carrying away into Babylon unto Christ are fourteen generations."

The Inner Meaning of Fourteen
The three subdivisions of the genealogy of Jesus, include first, the patriarchs and judges; second, the kings; and third, the priests. This number fourteen is made up of ten plus four, which being interpreted is *"the Decalogue of the Old Testament, and the Sacraments of the Four Gospels of the New." * * * "So in each of these periods (of fourteen) there is a great change, and in the last the old nature is dead, and Christ the New Man comes."

The First Great Change
It will be noticed that the first great change comes during the reign of David. This point will be quite clear to those who have carefully studied the previous chapters. David was not

---

*Chapters in Symbolism, by W. Frank Shaw, p. 115.

only the conqueror of Goliath the arch enemy of the soul, but he was the father of Solomon who built the Temple in Jerusalem.

The Second Great Change The Babylonian Captivity The second great change comes when the children of Israel are taken into captivity by the Assyrians; this is known as the Babylonian captivity. The children of Israel had been slaves in Egypt, but the bondage in Egypt under Pharaoh was quite different from that which they suffered while in Babylon. In Egypt they were in abject slavery, their bondage was grievous to be borne until Moses led them out from this land into the wilderness. We shall now ascertain how, after having once been delivered by God from this bondage, it was possible for them to be again taken captive. What then was the sin committed by the children of Israel? For it must always be remembered that it is the carnal mind, ignorance or sin, which enslaves us.

Before answering this question it might be well to state that there are four phases of this captivity.

The First Phase of the Captivity Let us consider the first phase. At this time Menahem, the son of Gadi, reigned over Israel, and

*"He did that which was evil in the sight of the Lord: he departed not all his days from the sins of Jeroboam."

What were the sins of Jeroboam?

It will be remembered that ten tribes of Israel had revolted from the sway of Rehoboam the son of Sol-

*II Kings, xv:18.

omon, leaving him to reign over the two tribes of Judah and Benjamin, and had formed a separate kingdom under Jeroboam the son of Nebat, "a mighty man of valour." Jeroboam, established on his throne, feared to allow his people to go up to sacrifice in the Temple at Jerusalem, lest they should return to their old allegiance, to Rehoboam King of Judah, and he himself should be deposed and slain. He made therefore two calves of gold and set up one of them in Bethel and the other in Dan. He made priests of the lowest of the people, those who were not of the sons of Levi, and offered sacrifices unto the calves.

Sacrificing in the Temple It should be remembered that Jerusalem is our consciousness, and that the temple is "the superstructure of Truth," the mental or spiritual structure which we are building. Sacrificing to God in the Temple at Jerusalem simply means that we are trying to realize Good as the only power, and that we are willing to make great sacrifices if need be; that we have the courage of our convictions, that we are following after the Truth, and that our chief desire is to love God with all our heart, soul, **Worshipping the Golden Calves** mind and strength. Worshipping the golden calves symbolizes the giving of power to matter and evil. We have disobeyed the first commandment—*"Thou shalt have none other gods before me," and we must suffer the consequences of our disobedience.

These two calves were set up in Bethel and Dan, and it might be helpful to ascertain the esoteric significance of these two names.

*Deuteronomy, v:7.

The Meaning *"In the city of Mecca * * * is a
of Bethel square edifice thirty feet high, called the
Kaabeh, or Cube. The Koran says it was the first
house of worship built for mankind. It has been known
from time immemorial as Beit-Allah, which name is the
exact equivalent of the Hebrew word Beth-El, (which
means) House of God. According to the Moslem
legend it was originally built by Adam, after the pat-
tern of a similar structure in Paradise, and was restored by Abraham. It contains a white stone,—now
blackened by time and by the kisses of pilgrims,—
which stone was also, according to tradition, brought
from Paradise. * * *

"The name Beth-El given to the Human House,
denotes that man, when 'cubic' or sixfold, is the habi-
tation of Deity."

Dan Defined Dan is derived from the Hebrew word
signifying "judge."

We know how man is the image and likeness of
God, and that Christ is in us. If we turn this temple
of God into a den of thieves, if we defile it and take
God's name in vain, if we both worship and fear evil,
thus believing in two opposite or warring powers—
then it is that we come to grief. God is the great
Judge, and this Judge is He who carries the balances in
His hand. Perfect balance is perfect justice, and it
should be remembered that justice and judgment are
one. God is Love, and hence He must also be just.
It is impossible then for man to escape the penalty
due for sin, since he literally punishes himself: his
slavery or captivity is the direct result of the infringe-

* The Perfect Way, by Anna Kingsford M. D., pp. 144-145.

ment of divine Law. If we wish to be free we must be careful not to set up golden calves in Bethel and Dan.

We now see the nature of Jeroboam's sins, and it was because King Menahem followed in his footsteps that *"Pul the king of Assyria came against the land." Pul, however, agreed with the king of Israel that if a war indemnity of one thousand talents of silver were paid, he would withdraw with his soldiers from the country. This sum Menahem exacted from the mighty men of wealth in Israel, obliging each man to pay fifty shekels of silver. The children of Israel were saved this first time by paying a sum of money to the king of Assyria, for since God is just and God is Love, we are not sorely punished for our first transgression.

The Inner Significance of Assyria   The literal translation of **Assyria** is plain or level. A plain signifies a low or material state of consciousness in contradistinction to **mount**, which denotes a state of spiritual exultation or illumination. The children of Israel, like all mortals, had not yet learnt their lesson. We are all more or less blind to sin, and frequently nothing but suffering will open our eyes.

The Second Phase of the Captivity   We now come to the second phase of the captivity.

The children of Israel continued to sin, and we read:

†"They caused their sons and their daughters to pass through the fire, and used divination and enchantments, and sold themselves to do evil

*II Kings, xv:19.
†II Kings, xvii:17, 18, 23.

. in the sight of the Lord, to provoke him to anger.

"Therefore the Lord was very angry with Israel, and removed them from out of his sight: there was none left but the tribe of Judah only.

. . . .

"So was Israel carried away out of their own land to Assyria unto this day."

The Lost Ten Tribes of Israel There has been much speculation as to what became of the ten tribes of Israel: they are frequently spoken of as the lost ten tribes. Certain investigators who call themselves Anglo-Israelites, have come to the conclusion after long and careful research that the English are actually the lost ten tribes! and many books have been written on this subject. But as far as can be seen, all the arguments are as futile and meaningless as the pathetic controversy between Professor Huxley and Mr. Gladstone.

What the Number Ten Symbolizes The number ten symbolizes divine Law or Principle: there are, for example, ten commandments; these the children of Israel had broken, and on the first occasion they were allowed to pay a thousand talents of silver—a thousand being the cube of ten. Ten is sometimes defined as "the number of perfection," and it is spoken of as "all complete" or "fully accomplished." Through practicing divination and necromancy the children of Israel found themselves in a confused and lawless state of mind; in other words, ten, or law, or the rule of divine Love had given place to confusion and captivity.

There are now only two tribes left, and in the place

of the ten tribes which were taken away, the Assyrians put their own people. But these aliens who now filled the cities of Samaria knew not God. Chaos reigned supreme, and we are told that lions slew them, because they knew not the manner of the God of the land.

The Twelve Tribes of Israel It might be well to state at this point that the twelve tribes of Israel represent twelve states or stages of consciousness— twelve compartments, shall we say, in the mind of man. These twelve tribes then are within each one of us. If we wilfully resist the love of God, we shall find that the lions will devour us. Here we have the inversion or perversion of that wonderful promise contained in the ninety-first Psalm, for instead of our trampling the lions under our feet they will devour us. The carnal mind is like a roaring lion and it is always opposed to the still small voice.

The Third Phase of the Captivity The third phase of the captivity is recorded in the twenty-fourth chapter of the second book of Kings.

*"Jehoiachin was eighteen years old when he began to reign, and he reigned in Jerusalem three months. * * *

"And he did that which was evil in the sight of the Lord, according to all that his father had done."

Therefore Nebuchadnezzar king of Babyon beseiged the city and "carried out thence all the treasures of the king's house, and cut in pieces all the ves-

*II Kings, xxiv:8, 9.

sels of gold which Solomon king of Israel had made in the temple of the Lord." All the princess and all the mighty men of valour were taken captive, also the craftsmen and smiths; and we have the signficant assertion that "none remained save the poorest sort of the people of the land."

Mental Degradation It must be remembered that Jehoiachin was king of Judah or the remaining two tribes, and through persisting in their sin they had descended into the very depths of mental degradation. This would be the interpretation of the statement that only the poorest sort of the people remained in the land. For the man who has seen the light, and yet persists in his sin, descends into greater depths of degradation than the man who sins through ignorance. The princes, craftsmen and smiths—the royal and constructive thoughts in our consciousness—are no longer building the temple, nor holding sway.

The Captivity in its Fourth Phase The sad account of the fourth phase of the Babylonian captivity is found in the twenty-fourth and twenty-fifth chapters of the book of II Kings, and reads as follows:

*"And the king of Babyon made Mattaniah his father's brother king in his stead, and changed his name to Zedekiah.

"Zedekiah was twenty and one years old when he began to reign, and he reigned eleven years in Jerusalem. * * *

"And he did that which was evil in the sight of the Lord, according to all that Jehoiakim had done.

*II King's, xxiv:17, 18-20, xxv:1, 2, 8-11, 21,22.

"For through the anger of the Lord it came to pass in Jerusalem and Judah, until he had cast them out from his presence, that Zedekiah rebelled against the king of Babylon.

"And it came to pass in the ninth year of his reign, in the tenth month, in the tenth day of the month, that Nebuchadnezzar king of Babylon came, he, and all his host, against Jerusalem, and pitched against it; and they built forts against it round about.

"And the city was besieged unto the eleventh year of king Zedekiah.

.   .   .   .

"So they took the king, and brought him up to the king of Babylon to Riblah; and they gave judgment upon him.

"And they **slew the sons of Zedekiah** before his eyes, and **put out the eyes of Zedekiah**, and **bound him with fetters of brass**, and carried him to Babylon.

"And in the fifth month, * * * came Nebuzarradan, captain of the guard, a servant of the king of Babylon; unto Jerusalem:

"And **he burnt the house of the Lord**, and **the king's house, and all the houses of Jerusalem**, and every great man's house burnt he with fire.

"And all the army of the Chaldees, that were with the captain of the guard, **brake down the walls of Jerusalem** round about.

"Now the rest of the people that were left in the city, and the fugitives that fell away to the king of Babylon, with the remnant of the multitude, did Nebuzaradan the captain of the guard carry away.

.   .   .   .

"So Judah was carried away out of their land.

"And as for the people that remained in the land of Judah, whom Nebuchadnezzar king of Babylon had left, even over them he made Gedaliah the son of Ahikam, the son of Shaphan, ruler."

Five Facts of Importance In the fourth phase of the captivity, the reader's attention is called to the following facts:

1—Zedekiah disobeyed the law of God, as his predecessors had done.

2—Jerusalem was destroyed in the eleventh year of Zedekiah's reign.

3—The king's sons were slain, his (the king's) eyes were put out and he was bound with fetters of brass.

4—"The house of the Lord, and the king's house, and all the houses of Jerusalem" were destroyed by fire, and the walls of the city were thrown down.

5—The inhabitants were carried away.

The above statements lead us to the conclusion that willful and persistent sin results in destruction and slavery in the eleventh year—the year of "transgression, iniquity, and sin, because it oversteps the Law of God." The final catastrophy may be postponed for a time, but its advent is inevitable if we persist in our sin.

Error's Offspring Destroyed Our sons are slain—in other words, the offspring of error are destroyed. Our eyes are put out, which is the destruction of spiritual perception; and our material senses are "five fetters" of brass.

Evil is Lawless Evil is destructive, since it has no law to govern it. If we do not build according to principle, the structures which we erect in consciousness, together with the wall surrounding them will be destroyed. Evil thoughts are no protection.

Man Enslaved by His Sinful Actions The sinner is thus a captive. "The people that were left in the city" were carried away, and man, in turn, will be enslaved by his sinful actions if he persists in them. What is the meaning of Babylon?

The Meaning of Babylon Doctor Young in his Concordance tells us that it is the God of Bel or confusion. No better word could be found to express that state of mind in which man finds himself when he gives way to this form of sin.

We have said that the number fourteen denotes a great change, and surely the state of the children of Israel at this period is nothing to be compared with their former prosperity and greatness. But through suffering they are gradually purified and eventually return to Jerusalem and rebuild the Temple. So it is with each one of us: if we do not learn our lesson through obeying the law of God, we are forced to learn it through suffering.

The Third Great Change From the time of the captivity we again ascend the ladder of life step by step through fourteen generations until we come to the third great change. Three, being the divine or perfect number, naturally culminates in the birth of Christ. But before passing on to this most fascinating subject, we will consider for a moment the story of the conception and birth of John the Baptist.

The Conception and Birth of John the Baptist   We read that Zacharias, Elizabeth's husband, was a priest and that his duty was to burn incense when he went into the Temple. The couple were well stricken in years, and they had no child. Zacharias, it might here be noted, symbolizes "remembered by Jehovah," and Elizabeth "God of the oath." We are also told that they were righteous before God, walking in all the commandments of the Lord blameless.

If we ever expect the beautiful Christ-idea to be immaculately conceived within us, it is exceedingly important that we should cultivate the Zacharias and Elizabeth thought. These thoughts when combined will give birth to a John the Baptist, who will prepare the way for the coming of the Christ-idea. This idea is no earthly thought, for we read that an angel appeared unto Zacharias and said:

*"Fear not, Zacharias: for thy prayer is heard; and thy wife Elizabeth shall bear thee a son, and thou shalt call his name John.

.   .   .   .

"For he shall be great in the sight of the Lord, and he shall drink neither wine nor strong

*Luke, 1:13, 15, 16.

drink; and he shall be filled with the Holy Ghost, even from his mother's womb.

"And many of the children of Israel shall he turn to the Lord their God."

We notice that Elizabeth hid herself for five months, and that "in the sixth month the angel Gabriel was sent from God * * * to a virgin espoused to a man whose name was Joseph, of the house of David." The definition of the two numbers five and six as previously given should be borne in mind at this point.

What John the Baptist Symbolizes John the Baptist was clothed in camel's hair, and his food was locusts and wild honey; he was likened to a voice crying in the wilderness.

Our consciousness is undoubtedly at this stage like a wilderness; and just as Moses lifted up his voice in Egypt and the wilderness against cruelty and oppression and sin, so John the Baptist is that thought which perceives that the coming of Christ is at hand: it cries out in the wilderness.

We should all cultivate this thought, for otherwise our consciousness will never be prepared for the birth of the Christ.

The Immaculate Conception It was the sixth month when the angel Gabriel appeared unto Mary and announced that "the power of the Highest" would "overshadow" her. He furthermore stated that it was now the sixth month with Elizabeth, who had conceived in her old age.

This holy thing to be born of Mary was to be called the Son of God.

God created man in His image on the sixth day, and we have already indicated how deeply significant is the six-pointed star or duoble triangle.

Jesus to Have Dominion Over all Things Material This immaculately conceived idea of God was to be named Jesus, and God promised to give him the throne of his father David, and the rulership over the house of Jacob for ever. In other words, Christ is to have dominion over the earth, over matter, and over the body for ever.

In St. Matthew's gospel we are told that the angel of the Lord appeared unto Joseph in a dream and said:

*"Joseph, thou son of David, fear not to take unto thee Mary thy wife: for that which is conceived in her is of the Holy Ghost.

"And she shall bring forth a son, and thou shalt call his name Jesus: for he shall save his people from their sins.

"Now all this was done, that it might be fulfilled which was spoken of the Lord by the prophet, saying,

"Behold, a virgin shall be with child, and shall bring forth a son, and they shall call his name Emmanuel, which being interpreted is, God with us."

Joseph and Mary are Types or Symbols Both Joseph and Mary are types or symbols, and thus it was quite natural that the angel should appear to both of these individuals, for spiritual or immaculate conception is not possible without the union of the masculine and feminine elements.

*St. Matthew. 1:20-23.

Mary now "went into the hill country with haste." This child of the Highest cannot breathe the oppressive material air of the lowlands or plains of "Assyria." He can thrive only in the hill country, in the rarified atmosphere of spiritual exaltation.

The Salutation of Mary Mary entered the house of Elizabeth and saluted her, and "when Elizabeth heard the salutation of Mary, the babe leaped in her womb." There is always a response where sympathy exists.

Christ would come to all of us, but the temple is not complete. We are down in Assyria, taken captive by the material senses, or perchance we are worshipping the golden calf in Bethel or in Dan. Eyes have we but we see not; ears we possess but there is no understanding. The angel messenger is requested to go his way and to come at a more convenient season: there is no sympathy, no response. The door is closed.

Love Calls Each Prodigal Son *"Except ye be converted, and become as little children, ye shall not enter into the kingdom of heaven." This tiny concept, John the Baptist, has not as yet been conceived by us. The healing oil, the saving Truth, are not for us as yet. Greater sacrifices are necessary before our blind eyes can see the light. How pathetic! But praise God from Whom all blessings flow, for one day all men will come to know and love this Child, since God is Love, and this Love will continue to call each prodigal son until he gladly returns to his Father's house, where there are many mansions.

*St. Matthew, xviii:3.

The Birth of Jesus   We read that Joseph and Mary went up to Bethlehem to be taxed and that while there, Mary *"brought forth her firstborn son, and wrapped him in swaddling clothes, and laid him in a manger."

Bethlehem is spoken of as the city of David.

Watch and Pray   It is significant that the angel of the Lord appeared unto the shepherds, and we should also notice that they were keeping watch over their flocks by night. Christ was the Son of David, and we have already indicated that David was a shepherd. Therefore it is only those who watch their wandering sheep, their thoughts, who will see this angel visitant, and hear his message. We must watch above all at night. When everything seems dark and dreary, and no light breaks through the gloom, it is then that we should be most watchful. The temptation for all is to get discouraged, and we often give up the fight just at the moment of victory. It is those then who watch and pray who are ready to hear the glad tidings of great joy: †"Unto you is born this day in the city of David a saviour, which is Christ the Lord."

The Cave of the Heart   This immaculately conceived idea was born in a stable or a cave, and this stable or cave is really the cave of the heart. During Christmas week in the Roman Catholic churches, particularly in the large cathedrals, it is customary for this scene to be pictured; and we usually find Joseph, Mary and the Child in the cave.

*Luke. ii:7.
†Luke. ii:11.

The Wise Men from the East Just as the shepherds saw the angel, so the Wise Men saw the star in the east. This star can never be perceived by those who have not constructed the Temple of Solomon—and Solomon is a master of wisdom. It is the wonderful combination of divine Wisdom and Love which gives birth to the Christ-idea. This star represents the heavenly or divine Light; and the Wise Men came from the east just as all that is pure and good must arise from that portion of our consciousness, as has been previously stated. Ezekiel tells us that *"the glory of the God of Israel came from the way of the east." These **The Gifts of Gold, Frankincense and Myrrh** Wise Men not only saw the star, but with joy and gratitude they sought for the young child in order that they might worship him and present their gifts of gold, frankincense and myrrh, thus showing that they recognized him as the king and priest who was to rise superior to death itself. Anna Kingsford informs us that †"their offerings of gold, frankincense, and myrhh denote the recognition of the indwelling divinity by the prophetic, priestly and regal attributes of man. Representing, respectively, the spirit, the soul, and the mind, they are symbolized as an angel, a queen, and a king; and they are, actually, Right Aspiration, Right Perception, and Right Judgment."

Heavenly Music At the birth of this child there was heavenly music. We read that a multitude of the heavenly host praised God, and this was only to be expected since the child was to bring peace on earth and goodwill to men. Nohting will ever bring greater

*Ezekiel. xliii:2.
†The Perfect Way. p. 238.

joy and peace to any human soul than this experience of the new birth, for it should be remembered, as previously stated, that Christ is in every man; and this must be so since man is God's image and likeness.

Christ's Birth Has a Threefold Significance The birth of Christ from an allegorical standpoint has three meanings: *"(1) the birth or appearance or manifestation of the Logos in matter through His Second Aspect; (2) the birth of the human soul, the ego, the individuality; and (3) the birth of the Christ-principle within the man at a later stage of his development."

Malice Against the Truth It is a remarkable thing, but nevertheless true, that no sooner is a beautiful idea conceived or born in one's consciousness than error tries either to crush or to kill it. In the case of Jesus we read that when the Wise Men told Herod that they had seen the star in the east, Herod inquired diligently of the details concerning the star and the child. Herod symbolizes the material king, the carnal mind, which is always opposed to Truth. Herod then was anxious to kill this child, but Truth is immortal and omnipotent, so all the carefully laid plans of the carnal mind came to naught, since evil has power only to destroy itself. It will be remembered that Herod had all the young children killed, but was not able to touch this child.

The Woman, the Man Child and the Dragon We find a parallel instance in the twelfth chapter of Revelation, where the woman clothed with the sun, and crowned with twelve stars gives birth to a male child.

*The Christian Creed, by C. W. Leadbeater, p. 76.

And the devil, the serpent or red dragon, was very wroth for he knew that his days were numbered.

> *"And the dragon stood before the woman which was ready to be delivered, for to devour her child as soon as it was born.
>
> "And she brought forth a man child, who was to rule all nations with a rod of iron: and her child was caught up unto God, and to his throne.
>
> .   .   .   .
>
> "And the serpent cast out of his mouth water as a flood after the woman, that he might cause her to be carried away of the flood.
>
> "And the earth helped the woman, and the earth opened her mouth, and swallowed up the flood which the dragon cast out of his mouth.
>
> "And the dragon was wroth with the woman, and went to make war with the remnant of her seed, which keep the commandments of God, and have the testimony of Jesus Christ."

God Protects His Own One of the first lessons to be learnt in connection with this Christian warfare is that there is nothing to fear, for God will always protect His own. It is worse than folly to fear evil, no matter what its guise may be. Neither the serpent nor the dragon can harm us so long as we are watchful. Herod was utterly thwarted in his diabolical scheme to kill the Christ, for the Wise Men were warned in a dream to return home by another way, and the Lord also appeared to Joseph and instructed him to take the young child and his mother down into Egypt, there to remain until the death of Herod.

*Revelation. xii:4, 5, 15, 16, 17.

The Significance of "Going Down Into Egypt" This going down into Egypt is very significant. As Christ is within, it is necessary for us to go down into Egypt; but this occasion is a very different one from that in which we were in bondage to Pharaoh. The object now is to put all enemies under our feet, and we only remain until this murderous Herod thought it utterly destroyed.

The Circumcision Jesus was circumcised on the eighth day. There is a deep spiritual meaning underlying this episode, and to gain the true significance of circumcision we will turn to the Old Testament and ascertain what Jeremiah has to say on the subject. The Lord addresses Himself to the men of Judah and Jerusalem, and advises them as follows:

> *"Break up your fallow ground, and sow not among thorns.
> "Circumcise yourselves to the Lord, and take away the foreskins of your heart, ye men of Judah and inhabitants of Jerusalem: * * * because of the evil of your doings."

In the New Testament the great mystic, St. Paul, offers us the key to this mystery when he says:

> †"Circumcision is that of the heart, in the spirit and not in the letter:

Again he says:

> ‡"Now I say that Jesus Christ was a minister of the circumcision for the truth of God."

And again:

*Jeremiah. iv:3, 4.
†Romans. ii:29.
‡Romans. xv:8.

*"In whom also ye are circumcised with the circumcision made without hands, in putting off the body of the sins of the flesh by the circumcision of Christ."

Circumcision a Spiritual Process It is evident then that we should eliminate or cut out of our lives, minds and hearts, everything that is fleshly, lustful and sensual. Christ comes as a purifying mental fire, burning away all the dross in our lower sense natures. It is, as St. Paul states, the "spirit" and not the "letter" which is so important. This circumcision is "made without hands." It has nothing whatever to do with earthly things; it is a heavenly or spiritual process, and we must be perpetually reminding ourselves that this heavenly kingdom is within the soul or consciousness of every human being. It should also be remembered that fallow ground is choked with weeds and thorns, so we must continually cultivate our subconscious carnal mind; otherwise it will become choked with evil thoughts. The life of a true Christian is one long warfare; the consciousness must be turned and overturned and each weed or evil thought quickly removed before it has an opportunity of going to seed. All this is essential to that man who would be spiritually and thus truly circumcised.

The Eighth Day It will be noted that circumcision took place on the eighth day. Symbolically speaking, eight is the number of "regeneration" and "resurrection." Eight is spoken of as "the first number that oversteps seven, the number of the old creation;" one might speak of it as the heavenly number,

*Colossians. ii:11.

for when old things have passed away and all things
have become new, we are in a heavenly state of consciousness. Note that the beatitudes are eight in number: it is marvelous how wonderfully consistent Scripture is, if interpreted correctly.

Jesus, the Carpenter's Son   Joseph was supposed to be a carpenter, for Jesus was spoken of as the carpenter's son. It is imperative that Christ
should be the son of a builder since he could not be
born until the temple had been constructed. Christ
is to complete the work initiated by his father, and
he must have assisted his father when a youth, for
we read that he was subject to his parents. Christ is
not only the son of a carpenter but is literally the chief
corner stone in the temple itself.

Jesus Disputing with the Doctors in the Temple   Christ's parents were wont to visit Jerusalem annually at the time of the Feast of the Passover, and it is recorded that when he was twelve years old he accompanied his parents thither.

At the close of the Feast his parents returned
home, but Jesus remained, disputing with the doctors
in the Temple, and asking them many questions. His
parents, missing Jesus, came back to Jerusalem in
search of him. When they found him they asked why
he had thus dealt with them, for he had made them
very sorrowful. His answer, as the answer of a boy
of twevle, may when looked at superficially seem dis-
respectful, for Jesus made it quite clear that now he
must "be about his Father's business." This Christ-
idea is to regenerate and transform all things; he is not

subject to the old conditions which by this time are outgrown. The Christ-mind is superior to all earthly wisdom.

His parents did not understand his reply. God's ways are always above our limited material understanding. But when the "still small voice" speaks it behooves us to listen, even though we may not fully comprehend the command. If we listen and obey, we shall "be about" our Father's business and our growth will be sturdy and rapid.

Twelve "the Number of the Incarnation" Christ was twelve years of age when he went up to Jerusalem. A study of the number twelve will help us to see more clearly why he went at that symbolical age. *"Twelve bears a similar relation to mankind that seven has to time, and four has to space; and this reference is one which belongs to mankind considered in union with God.

"In the highest sense twelve is the number of the Incarnation." Twelve tells us of an even "more intimate union" of man with the Father than does the number seven. It is not four added to three but four multiplied by three; and speaking symbolically, when numbers are multiplied the meaning is intensified.

The Baptism of Christ Our next step will be the baptism of Christ, but before considering this initiation in detail it will be well for us to remember that John the Baptist was preaching in the wilderness. It was his endeavor to prepare a straight and narrow way for the Christ. The statement that all the land

---

*Chapters on Symbolism by W. Frank Shaw, p. 102, (Quotation from Willis, p. 80).

of Judah and they of Jerusalem went out and were baptised in the river Jordan, confessing their sins, **A Preliminary** is pregnant with meaning. For, unless **Purification** we prepare the way for the coming of this Christ-idea, little can be done for us: we should be like individuals who are deaf, dumb and blind. The Spirit will cry out and plead with us, but there will be no response to its pleading. There is a certain preliminary purification which we must all experience before we can receive that higher illumination which we shall now elucidate. Observe in passing that from the birth of Christ to his baptism there was an interval **Definition of** of thirty years and six months. Mystic- **the Number** ally speaking, the number thirty repre- **Thirty** sents "maturity, manhood and reason." It is three multiplied by ten; in other words, man in in the image and likeness of the triune God governed by divine Law or Principle. There is sometimes a distinction made between the numbers thirty and thirty-one; the latter denotes what might be called the "final reward of heaven."

Joshua In our journey from sense to soul we **and the** come to milestones where we are re- **Thirty-One** warded. There is a particular instance **Kings** in Scripture where the number thirty-one lends itself to the interpretation given above. It is recorded that Joshua who led the children of Israel into the Promised Land, conquered and slew thirty-one kings before he finally gained possession of Canaan. Moses sent spies into the land of Canaan, and they returned with wonderful accounts of this country, saying it was a land flowing with milk and honey, but that there were giants there. This Moses thought is strong up to a point—it is strong enough to take us out of the land of Egypt, but it lacks that strength and courage which is so necessary for conquering the giants. It must die and give place to the Joshua thought before we can enter the Promised Land. On three different occasions the Lord commanded Joshua to be strong and of a good courage; and living up to this command, he obtained his reward. The thirty-one kings slain by Joshua might be likened to thirty-one giants; and until we are able to master these giants, we are in no position to receive that glorious reward which divine Love is ready and willing to bestow upon us. "Justice is the handmaid of mercy," and one of the first lessons that man must learn is that he will never gain something for nothing. Without justice the universe would be chaotic.

The baptism is that final reward; it is the consummation of that epoch or period in Christ's life, represented by the number thirty-one.

What is this reward?

The Baptism of Water, of the Holy Ghost, and of Fire John the Baptist said that he baptised with water, but Christ who was to follow after him would baptise with the Holy Ghost and with fire. A most beautiful and helpful passage on this subject is found in "The Perfect Way."

*"Intuition, is completed and crowned by the operation of Divine Illumination. Theoretically, this illu-

*The Perfect Way, by Anna Kingsford, M.D., pp. 3, 4.

mination is spoken of as the Descent of the Holy Spirit, or outpouring of the heavenly efflux, which kindles into a flame in the soul, as the sun's rays in a lens. Thus, to the fruits of the soul's experience in the past, is added the 'grace' or luminance of the Spirit;—the baptism of Fire which, falling from on high, sanctifies and consummates the results of the baptism of Water springing from the earth."

The Partial Rending of the Veil When this stage on our heavenly journey is reached we are prepared for the great illumination; the fire now burns brightly in the soul consuming the dross of sin and ignorance. Baptism is not only the purification and the forgiveness of sin through the destruction of sin, but also the partial rending of the veil of the temple. Man begins to see things more clearly and this is truly an initiation; to him it is now given to know some of the mysteries of the kingdom of heaven. This fire with which Jesus was baptised comes from heaven; in other words, from Spirit and not from matter. The Buddhist acknowledges "one initiation for the casting off of the fetters." Now the forgiveness of sin is really emancipation from sin, for nothing fetters man like sin. It is a heavy yoke, whereas Christ's yoke is easy and his burden is light. God is well pleased with the initiate who reaches this stage of development. It is recorded that the heavens were opened and that the Spirit of God descended upon Christ like a dove, and there was a voice from heaven saying: *"This is my beloved Son, in whom I am well pleased."

*St. Matthew, III :17.

Preparatory Cleansing The baptism of John is essential, as there is a great deal of preparatory cleansing to be done before this divine illumination can become an assured fact.

The Temptation We now come to one of the most significant episodes in Christ's life, for it is stated that immediately after the baptism he was led of the Spirit into the wilderness to be tempted of the devil. It has been said that *"the higher Truth lifts her voice, the louder will error scream, until its inarticulate sound is forever silenced in oblivion." A man cannot make a thing his own until he has been tested and tried; mere faith is not sufficient, he must know; that is, he must be able to demonstrate this knowledge every step of the way. It was necessary then that the Christ should be tried. A man who is unable to withstand temptation is not justified in considering that he has this Christ-like understanding.

Why Temptation Follows Illumination The question now arises: Why should temptation follow immediately upon illumination? Can it be possible that light can produce darkness, and is it literally true that God tempts man?

†"Let no man say when he is tempted, I am tempted of God: for God cannot be tempted with evil, neither tempteth he any man:

"But every man is tempted, when he is drawn away of his own lust, and enticed.

"Then when lust hath conceived, it bringeth .

*Science and Health, by Mary Baker Eddy, p. 97.
†St. James, 1:13-15.

forth sin: and sin when it is finished, bringeth
forth death."

We see that it is impossible for God to tempt any
man, and yet it is a fact that this divine illumination
or fire which burns brightly in the soul of man seems
to stir up evil which is now ripe for destruction. We
have referred to the fallow ground filled with thorns,
and this reminds me of an asparagus bed with which I
had some difficulty a few years ago.

Evil Comes This bed had been neglected for a long
to the Surface time, the ground having been neither fer-
Ripe for
Destruction tilized nor tilled. I manured it thoroughly and turned over the soil. When
the warm sunny days of spring arrived I found that
instead of asparagus, thistles and weeds grew apace.
The very fertilizer which had been intended for the
asparagus nourished the thistles. However, as fast as
the weeds appeared I pulled them out, so that none of
them might go to seed. On turning over the soil more
thistle seeds were brought to the surface, and they
produced in turn another crop of weeds. But it only
required patience during the first season, practically
to exterminate the weeds, and the second year I received the fruit of all my labours. Right thinking and
right desire undoubtedly bring evil to the surface, but
rather than lament that this evil appears, one should
rejoice that it comes up to the surface to be destroyed.
It is in the darkened consciousness that evil lurks, not
in the mind which has been illuminated by divine
Light.

Not a Sin to be Tempted Again, bear in mind that it is not a sin to be tempted, for it is recorded that Jesus was in all points tempted like as we are, yet without sin.

The three temptations of Jesus are interesting and significant.

"Man Shall Not Live by Bread Alone" In the first the devil suggests that Jesus should command that the stones be made bread; but the Christ was too wise to fall a prey to this subtle temptation. The reply he made to the tempter was the essence of wisdom: ..*"Man shall not live by bread alone, but by every word that proceedeth out of the mouth of God." The time will come when we shall all realize that the things of this world do not satisfy: nothing of a material nature can really feed the soul; the things of time and sense are dust and ashes; †"vanity of vanities, saith the preacher; all is vanity." The real and eternal is the spiritual; and the more we feed on spiritual thoughts the greater is our satisfaction.

The Second Temptation We are not to let Satan persuade us to cast ourselves down from a pinnacle of the temple,—the second temptation—even though we have the promise in the ninety-first Psalm that God will give His angels charge over us to keep us in all our ways.

Mad Ambition, and the Abuse of Spiritual Power In the third temptation the devil suggested to Jesus that he should use his great powers to his own personal advantage. It is always a dangerous thing for an unscrupulous or impure mind to be in

*St. Matthew, iv:4.
†Ecclesiastes, xii:8.

possession of power. The higher we rise the lower we fall if we are so foolish or so shortsighted as to yield to this temptation. This last temptation was really the evil suggestion from the devil or the carnal mind, tempting Christ to give way to mad ambition. Selfishness can never bring happiness. One of the first laws or commandments laid down by Christ is: *"He that loseth his life for my sake shall find it." It is only by giving that we receive, and when the divine Light burns brightly in our souls we must then so use it that it will heal the sin-sick and broken-hearted.

The Milestone of Resisted Temptation   Having reached in our journey this milestone of resisted temptation, we are now in the position to help humanity spiritually, mentally, morally and physically; and if we use aright the talents that God has given us, then since Love is the fulfilling of the law, we shall rise to sublime heights. Just as Jesus dealt with these evil thoughts and suggestions, so we must deal with them day by day. We must say literally with him: †"Get thee hense, Satan: for it is written, Thou shalt worship the Lord thy God, and him only shalt thou serve."

The Wilderness Defined   It was in the wilderness that Jesus was tempted. The wilderness represents that state of consciousness in which we are tried. If we are proof against evil thoughts, then the angels or heavenly messengers will flood our consciousness with peace and joy.

*St. Matthew, x:39.
†St. Matthew, iv:10.

The Marriage Feast After this great illumination followed by the temptation in the wilderness, we are prepared for the marriage feast in Cana of Galilee, when we are wedded to Truth and Love. We then feel that sense of unity which is so essential to the Christian knight or warrior: the soul, in other words, must be wedded to the "divine spirit of the man."

What is Wine? The water which purified us can now be turned into wine or inspiration. What is this wine? It is the fruit of the vine, and Christ said: *"I am the vine, ye are the branches." It is when the Christ Truth wells up within us, enabling us to bear fruit in the form of loving thoughts, words and deeds, that we are truly inspired.

The following citations further elucidate the meaning of the marriage, and the turning of water into wine:

The Inner Significance of Marriage †"To be regenerate is to be born into spiritual life, and to have united the individual will with the Divine Will.

"The union of the two wills constitutes the spiritual marriage, the accomplishment of which is in the Gospels represented under the parable of the marriage of Cana of Galilee. This divine Marriage, or union of the human and Divine Wills, is indissoluble; whence the idea of the indissolubility of human marriage. And inasmuch as it is a marriage of the spirit of man to that of God, and of the Spirit of God to that of man, it is a double marriage."

‡" 'The fire of the soul must be kept alive by the Divine Breath, if it is to live for ever. It must con-

*St. John. xv:5.
†Clothed with the Sun, by Anna Kingsford. M. D., p. 91.
‡The Bible's Own Account of Itself, by Edward Maitland, p. 42.

verge, not diverge. If it diverge it will be dissipated. The end of progress is unity; the end of degradation is division. The soul, therefore, which ascends, tends more and more to union with the Divine.' This, the final state of the soul, is described in the Apocalypse under the figure of a marriage, wherein the contracting parties are the soul herself and the now divine spirit of the man, which is called the 'Lamb.'"

The Six Water Pots It will be observed that there were six water pots. This is the third significant occasion on which this number has been employed in connection with man. He was created on the sixth day, Mary conceived in the sixth month, and at his marriage feast there are six jars filled with water.

From the date of this marriage Christ began to work miracles: to heal the sick, to cleanse the lepers, to forgive sins and to raise the dead. No miraculous or marvelous thing can be performed till man is at-one with the Father which is in heaven.

A Long Journey, but a Glorious Reward This has been a long journey with many footsteps sometimes seemingly painful, but the glorious reward is well worth every effort put forth by the student or initiate, and although, like Jacob, we may be at the foot of this heavenly ladder, our head resting on a pillow of stone, nevertheless it is helpful for us to get even a glimpse of this far-off heavenly vision, for in reality it is here and now: heaven is both within us and at hand. Therefore it behooves us to move steadily forward, step by step, looking to God daily for wisdom and strength, never looking behind us, but keeping our eyes fixed on the star of Love. If we do this we are sure to conquer since God is true to His promises: He is unchanging Wisdom and Love.

CHAPTER V.

AT-ONE-MENT

The Periods or Divisions of Christ's Life Before dealing with the special footsteps which lead to the final at-one-ment, or that stage at which Jesus declared, "It is finished," we shall review the periods or divisions of Christ's life.

The particular phases dealt with in the previous chapter might be placed under two great divisions: the first treating of that period of his life beginning with his birth and closing with the ministry of John the Baptist, covering altogether about thirty years and six months; and the second beginning with Jesus' baptism and concluding with the marriage feast in Cana of Galilee. This latter covers no more than six months of his life.

The Five Subdivisions to be Considered in This Chapter That part of Christ's career with which in this chapter we shall deal is divided into five parts or subdivisions. The first begins with Jesus' visit to the city of Capernaum where he remained a few days, after which he went up to Jerusalem for the Passover, and while there cast the traders out of the temple. This subdivision covers a period of twelve months.

The second opens at the time of the Passover with the healing of an infirm man at Bethesda in Jerusalem, and extends over twelve months.

The third begins with Jesus' discourse with the pharisees and scribes in the presence of the disciples and a multitude of people, his subject being the eating with unwashed hands. This division also extends over twelve months, and concludes with the "transactions on the fourth day of the week in which Jesus was crucified."

The fourth embraces three days only, beginning with the preparations for keeping the Passover—and it should be noted that this was the fourth time that he prepared for the Passover. This division ends with the day before the resurrection.

The fifth and last concludes that period of time beginning with the day of the resurrection and closing with Christ's ascension: this covers a period of forty days.

Christ Completes His Perfect Work in Three Years and Three Days The three years and three days, which is the total length of time embodied in the first four divisions, is most significant when we bear in mind the meaning of the number three—the divine number. Christ completes his divine or perfect work during these three years and three days, which time closes with the killing-out or the death of the old man Adam.

The Inner Meaning of Three and One-Half Years There is a very interesting period in Christ's life which begins with his baptism and concludes with the "transactions on the fourth day of the week in which he was crucified." This covers three years

and six months. These three and a half years are
sometimes spoken of in Scripture as 1260 days, on
other occasions as forty-two months, and again as time,
times, and half a time.

It will be noticed that the 1260 days are produced
by multiplying 360 by 3½, 360 degrees being the number of degrees in a circle and representing the complete
circle or cycle of time. Again, 3½ is just the half of 7
or the position midway between 1 and 7. It denotes
"present suffering to be followed by future rest and
joy," and symbolizes "times of trouble." It covers the
whole of Jesus' ministry, namely, from the baptism to
the fourth Passover, during which time he was tempted
of the devil and in turn cast devils out of those with
whom he came in contact; healed the sick and the sinful, and raised the dead.

Excerpts from This number forty-two is most significant
Daniel and when we realize the scattering of the
Revelation power of the holy people mentioned by
Daniel (xii:7) which continued for a "time, times, and
half a time."

Again, in the eleventh chapter of Revelation:—
    *"The holy city shall they tread under foot
forty and two months.

"And I will give power unto my two witnesses, and they shall prophesy a thousand two
hundred and threescore days, clothed in sack-
cloth.

"These are the two olive trees, and the two
candlesticks standing before the God of the
earth.

*Revelation. xi:2, 3, 4, 5, 8, 9, 11.

"And if any man will hurt them, fire proceedeth out of their mouth, and devoureth their
enemies.

.   .   .   .   .   .

"And their dead bodies shall lie in the street
of the great city, which spiritually is called
Sodom and Egypt, where also our Lord was
crucified.

"And they of the people and kindreds and
tongues and nations shall see their dead bodies
three days and a half, and shall not suffer their
dead bodies to be put in graves.

.   .   .   .   .   .

"And after three days and a half the spirit
of life from God entered into them, and they
stood upon their feet; and great fear fell upon
them which saw them."

The Olive Trees and the Two Witnesses   The olive trees, mentioned in the above
citation, give us the healing balm or oil—
that oil which the elders were to use in
anointing the head of the sick. The two
witnesses are also spoken of as two candlesticks.
These, of course, hold the light; and it will be remembered that Christ said: *"Ye are the light of the
world. A city that is set on an hill cannot be hid."
So it can be seen that this divine Light, this healing oil,
stands before the God of the earth for 1260 days, or
until such time as evil is destroyed.

In the twelfth chapter of Revelation we read that
the woman who †"brought forth a man child * * *
fled into the wilderness, where she hath a place pre-

*St. Matthew, v:14.
†Revelation, xii:5, 6.

pared of God, that they should feed her there a thousand two hundred and threescore days." Following this we have the significant statement that there was war in heaven and that Michael and his angels fought against the dragon.

The Number Forty Defined It might be asked why the time which elapsed between the resurrection and the ascension was spoken of as forty days. The answer is that forty is the number symbolizing "waiting, probation, and purification." It is also defined as the period of "our sojourn here below."

Instances in Scripture Where the Number Forty Appears There are several significant instances in which this number forty appears in Scripture. The flood lasted for forty days. The Israelites wandered in the wilderness for forty years. Moses was in Egypt for forty years. Moses and Elijah fasted in the wilderness for forty days. Joshua had to wait until he was forty years of age before he was appointed to the leadership of the Israelites. As a punishment for their sins the Lord delivered the children of Israel into the hands of the Philistines for forty years. Goliath proved the men of Israel for forty days. Mary and Joseph waited for forty days before they presented Christ in the Temple at Jerusalem. Christ fasted in the wilderness forty days. In each of the above instances we see that the number forty is symbolical of "waiting, probation, and purification."

It will be interesting to study the different Passovers which Jesus attended. Of the first when he was twelve years old, we have already spoken. The

The Different Passovers Attended by Jesus second took place immediately after the marriage feast in Cana of Galilee. On this occasion he found the Temple filled with money changers and them that sold sheep and oxen and doves. And he drove them out. **The Temple Purified** This Temple, as has been stated, is our consciousness, and it is absolutely essential that everything of this nature should be driven out before we can attain to any degree of purity. Spiritual progress can never be made so long as we convert this Temple into "an house of merchandise."

A year hence Jesus again attends the Passover. We read in the fifth chapter of St. John's Gospel:

*"There was a feast of the Jews; and Jesus went up to Jerusalem."

Jesus Heals a Helpless Invalid This cleansing process which was begun a year ago is continued, and what happened at this time is most significant. We find that at Jerusalem by the sheep market there was a pool called Bethesda, "having five porches." "In these lay a great multitude of impotent folk." We are further told that at certain periods an angel troubled the waters and whoever stepped into the pool first was healed. On this occasion a man who had been helpless for thirty-eight years was waiting for the troubling of the waters, and Jesus said unto him: "Rise, take up thy bed and walk." The man was healed immediately. Our consciousness when it is filled with a multitude of impotent folk, has five porches, and only the Christ can heal and purify it.

*St. John. v:1-9.

Another year elapses, and we read in the fifteenth chapter of St. Matthew:

"Then came to Jesus scribes and Pharisees, which were of Jerusalem, saying,

"Why do thy disciples transgress the tradition of the elders? for they wash not their hands when they eat bread.

"But he answered and said unto them, Why do ye also transgress the commandment of God by your tradition?"

Hypocrisy Condemned He upbraided them for their hypocrisy and quoted Esaias against them: *"This people draweth nigh unto me with their mouth, and honoureth me with their lips; but their heart is far from me."

It should be observed that on the first occasion the money changers were cast out; on the second, disease; and on the third, hypocrisy. The consciousness has thus become purer.

The Transfiguration The transfiguration on the mount, which happens during this period, is defined as that experience "where the inner Deity shines through." Man must eventually so purify his mind that it becomes transparent. The windows of the soul must be cleaned of evil thoughts, for every evil thought defiling the mind is like a spot of mud defiling a window pane. The consciousness of mortals must be cleansed with the water of Life and purified by the Fire from heaven.

Christ had already been baptised; he had also attended, after his public ministry had begun, his third

*St. Matthews. xv:1. 2. 3. 8.

Passover at Jerusalem. The multitude had also been miraculously fed by him with bread and fish. These are all prepatory steps leading up to the transfiguration.

Jesus Prepared His Disciples for the Coming Transfiguration The sixteenth chapter of St. Matthew should be carefully studied before the story of the transfiguration is read (particularly verses 13, 16, 17, 20 and 21) because it shows us how Jesus also prepared his disciples for the coming transfiguration.

*"He asked his disciples, saying, Whom do men say that I the Son of man am?

.   .   .

"And Simon Peter answered and said, Thou art the Christ, the Son of the living God.

"And Jesus answered and said unto him, Blessed art thou, Simon Bar-jona: for flesh and blood hath not revealed it unto thee, but my Father which is in heaven."

Here we have in substance the same declaration that was made later at the time of the transfiguration, for we read:

†"And after six days Jesus taketh Peter, James, and John his brother, and bringeth them up into an high mountain apart,

"And he was transfigured before them: and his face did shine as the sun, and his raiment was white as the light.

.   .   .   .   .   .

*St. Matthew, xvi :13, 16, 17.
†St. Matthew, xvii :1, 2, 5.

"A bright cloud overshadowed them: and behold a voice out of the cloud, which said, This
is my beloved Son, in whom I am well pleased;
hear ye him."

"Into an High Mountain" The reader should notice that Jesus took
his disciples, not on to but "into" a high
mountain. This "high mountain" is an
exalted state of consciousness—the same mountain
"into" which Jesus went when he preached his sermon
on the mount, and Moses went to receive the ten commandments of the law.

The Fourth and Last Passover We now turn to the *fourth and last
Passover which Jesus kept with his dis-
ciples. The disciples inquired of the
Master where this Passover was to be eaten, for they
wished to make preparation. Jesus told them to go
to the city where they would meet a man bearing a
pitcher of water; they were to follow him, and he
would lead them to a large upper room furnished. In
this room they were to make ready.

The Man Bearing the Pitcher of Water It is always the man bearing the pitcher
of water on his head that will lead us to
this upper chamber. The man would
naturally carry the water on his head, for
the head is the seat of intelligence, and man as God's
image and likeness reflects divine Intelligence. We
are distinctly told that we must have that mind in us
which was in Christ Jesus.

The water in the pitcher is similar to that of the
brook out of which David selected his stones, and to

*St. Luke, xxii.

the water drawn from the well that Jesus spoke of as "living water;" it is "still water;" also the water of that river of life on whose banks the tree of life was planted.

When we bear a pitcher of water on our heads we are in an exalted state of consciousness; we must follow this thought and ascend the spiral stairway to the upper chamber—the winding stairs in Solomon's temple. In this chamber we eat the flesh and drink the blood, in other words we partake of bread and wine at the Last Supper—the Lord's Supper.

The Lord's Supper and the First Passover What connection is there between this Last Supper and the first Passover mentioned in Exodus? For there is a connection, since Christ distinctly commanded his disciples to make preparation for the keeping of the Passover.

The Tenth Plague in Egypt It will be remembered that the tenth plague in Egypt was the killing of the firstborn of the Egyptians.

*"And all the firstborn in the land of Egypt shall die, from the firstborn of Pharaoh that sitteth upon his throne, even unto the firstborn of the maidservant that is behind the mill; and all the firstborn of beasts.

.   .   .   .

"But against any of the children of Israel shall not a dog move his tongue, against man or beast: that ye may know how that the Lord doth put a difference between the Egyptians and Israel."

*Exodus. xi:5, 7.

The Dog a Symbol of Evil The dog here represents evil thought: in Revelation he is associated with sorcerers, whoremongers, and murderers, idolators, and "whosoever loveth and maketh a lie." None of these things, however, can touch the children of Israel."

The Blood of the Lamb In the twelfth chapter of Exdous we are told that *"the Lord spake unto Moses and Aaron in the land of Egypt, saying, This month shall be unto you the beginning of months: it shall be the first month of the year to you." They were further commanded to take very man a lamb on the tenth day of this month. This lamb was to be a male without blemish of the first year. Again the interesting number fourteen was used. We are told that the lamb was to be kept until the fourteenth day of the same month, when it was to be killed in the evening. This, of course, signified that some great change was to occur. They were told to eat unleavened bread with bitter herbs; to gird their loins, and to have their staff in their hand and shoes on their feet. God said, "Against all the gods of Egypt I will execute judgment: I am the Lord." They were further instructed to take the blood and to strike it on the two side posts and on the upper door post of their houses.

†"And ye shall take a bunch of hyssop, and dip it in the blood that is in the bason, and strike the lintel and the two side posts with the blood that is in the bason; and none of you shall go out at the door of his house until the morning."

*Exodus, xii:1, 2.
†Exodus, xii:22.

The Lord said that this was to be called "The Lord's Passover."

Do not forget that the firstborn of the Egyptians, including the firstborn of cattle, were killed at midnight.

We are told in the New Testament that a lamb should be killed, for we read: *"Behold the Lamb of God, which taketh away the sin of the world," and Christ is that Lamb.

The Inner Meaning of Blood   The blood of the lamb was to be sprinkled on the door post, and this blood is the cleansing, healing and protecting power; it is verily the life of Christ, and the door of our consciousness must be sprinkled with this Christ-life. The two door posts may be likened to two sentinels. When the sentinels are on duty it is impossible for the angel of death to enter, since God is Life, and "Christ is the divine manifestation of God."

The Divine Fire   The Israelites were to eat the lamb after it had been roasted in the fire. God is the divine Fire which removes all dross from the consciousness of man.

Life a Seeming Paradox   This lamb was to be eaten with bitter herbs. In the book of Revelation the little book with seven seals is described as sweet as honey in the mouth, but bitter in the belly. Life is a seeming paradox, for what seems to the carnal consciousness bitter, will in the end lead us onward and upward to a state of consciousness that is sweet as honey. The sacrificing or burning away of the

*St. John. 1:29.

error may at times be a most painful process, but deep down in the consciousness of man there is a stillness, a peace, a joy and a sweetness transcending all earthly joys: these neutralize all that is bitter in life. Divine Love truly meets every need: it is the universal solvent, the philosopher's stone, the universal panacea, the elixir of life.

Feet Shod, Loins Girded, and Staff in Hand Not only is it necessary to have blood sprinkled on our door posts: we must also have our loins girded, our shoes on our feet, and a staff in our hand. In speaking of the armour of God, St. Paul says, *"And your feet shod with the preparation of the gospel of peace." The staff is really a divining rod. The psalmist sings: †"Thy rod and thy staff they comfort me." This rod, when it is thrown to the earth, is turned into a serpent and swallows up all the divining rods of the carnal mind. ‡"For they cast down every man his rod, and they became serpents: but Aaron's rod swallowed up their rods."

Remain on Guard When Error is Rampant The children of Israel were to remain in their houses until the morning. During the night when error is rampant we must always remain on guard. We have referred to the fact that the firstborn of the Egyptians were killed at midnight. Now, night is typical of death, destruction and mental darkness, whereas day and light symbolize life, progression and all that is beautiful and good.

*Ephesians, vi:15.
†Psalms, xxiii:4.
‡Exodus, vii:12.

The Passover and the Lord's Supper Compared In comparing this Passover with the Lord's Supper, we notice that in the Passover the Egyptians or carnal thoughts were destroyed; (the firstborn of the Egyptians) and after it all the Egyptians were drowned in the Red Sea, while the Israelites passed safely through this red error: and that after the Lord's Supper Christ was to be crucified, and thus was to rise above all material things. It was, however, the fleshly, carnal self alone that was to be crucified, for that which is good can never be destroyed. It is the putting off of the "old man" with his deeds.

At the Passover there was the eating of the flesh, after it had been roasted in the fire, and the unleavened bread. At the Lord's Supper, the disciples were given bread and wine. We read:

*"That the Lord Jesus the same night in which he was betrayed took bread:

"And when he had given thanks, he brake it, and said, Take, eat: this is my body, which is broken for you: this do in remembrance of me.

"After the same manner also he took the cup, when he had supped, saying, This cup is the new testament in my blood: this do ye, as oft as ye drink it, in remembrance of me.

"For as often as ye eat this bread, and drink this cup, ye do shew the Lord's death till he come."

Shortly after the Passover the children of Israel were led out of the land of Egypt, or out of gross bondage to the material senses, across the Red Sea,

*I Corinthians. xi:23-26.

eventually into the promised land; and in like manner, to use St. Paul's language, as often as we eat the flesh (bread) and drink the blood (cup) we "do shew the Lord's death till he come." Christ must come to us **Daily** all, and if we daily eat this flesh and **Communion** drink his blood, our consciousness will become purified—a fit temple for the indwelling of divine Love. Man should thus commune with God daily, yea, hourly; it is not enough to partake of the material symbol once a week or at longer intervals. We should indeed, as the Bible commands, pray or commune with God without ceasing.

*"For the bread which is broken and divided for the children of the Kingdom is the Divine Substance, which with the Wine of the Spirit, constitutes the Holy Sacrament of the Eucharist, the Communion of the Divine and the Terrene, the Oblation of Deity in Creation.

"May this holy Body and Blood, Substance and Spirit, Divine Mother and Father, inseparable Duality in Unity, given for all creatures, broken and shed, and making oblation for the world, be everywhere known, adored, and venerated! May we, by means of that Blood, which is the Love of God and the Spirit of Life, be redeemed, indrawn, and transmuted into that Body which is Pure Substance, immaculate and ever virgin, express image of the Person of God."

The Agony After the Last Supper we come to the **in the** agony in the garden. Jesus took with him **Garden** his three trusted disciples, Peter, James and John; and we are told that he became "exceeding

*The Perfect Way, by Anna Kingsford, M.D., pp. 115-116.

sorrowful, even unto death." He prayed to his Father that the cup might pass from him. This is indeed a critical moment in the life of the Christ. The carnal mind struggles with the higher spiritual self for supremacy. But there is nothing to fear, even at this point, for Christ is to put all enemies under his feet. And although with one breath he prayed to have the cup removed, yet with the next he uttered the desire to bow to his Father's will. The suffering is as nothing compared with the joys prepared for those who have washed their robes white in the blood of the Lamb. At this stage of our spiritual development we are to be tempted and tried to the utmost.

Alone with God During this agony of the Christ, his trusted disciples and even the disciple he loved most, John, fell asleep, and he was alone. We will all eventually realize that the greatest happiness, freedom and spirituality can only be attained by passing through this experience—by being alone with God. We must learn to rise above human sympathy and human support. This step is, of course, one of the last steps in our spiritual development, in our long journey from sense to soul, from matter to spirit; but it must **True Love and Sympathy Essential** be taken. It does not mean, however, that we are not to be sympathetic and loving in the right way. Neither are we to refuse sympathy, but rather to avoid "Job's comforters." Christ was the very essence of love, and he devoted his whole life to healing the broken-hearted, the sin-sick, the maimed, the dumb and the blind, and to raising the dead. Yet, in spite of this, it was necessary for him to make this wonderful demonstration; and we know that, if he was able to survive what seems to us at times a sorrow almost too great to be borne, we can walk fearlessly in his footsteps; all the initial steps, however, must be taken. Christ is the Way, the Truth, and the Life; and we must fearlessly follow him like little children.

The Final Struggle Followed by Peace   Three times Christ prayed that the cup might be taken from him, but at last he was at peace; the great struggle had ceased; he was able to rise above the evidence of his material senses, to enter his closet and shut his door, and to pray to his Father in secret—in the holy of holies. Nothing can either harm or daunt those who are at-one with their Father in heaven.

The High Priest's Servant Healed   After Gethsemane this peace which floods the soul of the Christ like a river, is so profound, these thoughts that fill his mind are so far above the things of this world, that even the ear of the high priest's servant can be healed. This scene is a most impressive one. The band of men and officers from the chief priests, with their lanterns and torches and weapons coming to seize the Christ, quickly disturbs Peter: he draws his sword and cuts off the ear of the high priest's servant. But nothing can destroy the God-given calm of the Christ. When man reaches this stage in his development, evil is absolutely impotent.

Christ is spoken of as a king and as a priest, and we are told that we are all to be kings and priests unto God. Bearing this in mind, it is interesting to observe

Christ Brought Before Pontius Pilate and the High Priest that Christ during his trial is brought before Pontius Pilate and the high priest; in other words, the spiritual king and priest is tried by the earthly king and priest. The outer animal consciousness is continually judging the inner spiritual man: and this is inevitable since the carnal mind *"is not subject to the law of God"—a law to which it is opposed, and which it is not capable of understanding. This lower animal self with its multitude of raging, sensual thoughts cries out, "Crucify him, crucify him." The wise man is he who, like the Christ, holds his **Love Your Enemies** peace under the severest provocation. By the help of divine Love, this wise man can be calm, yea, he can even love his enemies, though he be scourged and mocked, clothed in a purple robe, and crowned with thorns. He can even stand the indignity of being spat upon. The judgments of this world can never harm the Christ Truth; it is indestructible and above all mokery and scorn, but the Judas who betrays the Truth will go out and hang himself. Evil is its own executioner.

The Crucifixion In considering the crucifixion, there are three significant passages which should be carefully studied. The first is in the sixth chapter of Romans:

†"Therefore we are buried with him by baptism into death: that like as Christ was raised up from the dead by the glory of the Father, even so we also should walk in newness of life.

*Romans, viii:7.
†Romans, vi:4-7.

"For if we have been planted together in the likeness of his death, we shall be also in the likeness of his resurrection:

"Our Old Man is Crucified" "Knowing this, that our old man is crucified with him, that the body of sin might be destroyed, that henceforth we should not serve sin.

"For he that is dead is freed from sin."
The second is in the fifth chapter of Galatians:

Crucify the Flesh *"And they that are Christ's have crucified the flesh with the affections and lusts."
The third is in Revelation, the eleventh chapter:

The Great City Spiritually Called Sodom and Egypt †"And their dead bodies shall lie in the street of the great city, which spiritually is called Sodom and Egypt, where also our Lord was crucified."

The Evolution of the Cross It might be well at this point to explain the evolution of that most ancient of all symbols, the cross. The meaning underlying this symbol is so profound and significant that one might say it is the centre of all symbols. To understand the deeper meaning of the crucifixion one must comprehend each stage in the development of the cross.

The ancients, when symbolizing the Absolute, used the circle or disc.

What is known as ‡"the first differentiation in the

---

*Galatians, v:24.
†Revelation, xi:8.
‡The Secret Doctrine, by H. P. Blavatsky, Vol. I, p. 34.

periodical manifestations of the ever-eternal Nature, sexless and infinite" is symbolized by a point within a circle .

The cross reaches its third stage of development when the circle is divided into two equal parts by a straight line; this symbolizes the divine Motherhood or what is sometimes termed *"a divine immaculate Mother-Nature within the all-embracing absolute Infinitude."

The next step in the development of the cross within the circle is a second line or diameter crossing the first at right angles, thus dividing the circle into four equal parts.

Mr. Leadbeater in his "Christian Creed" beautifully expresses this portion of the development as follows:

Emblems of the Unfolding of the Triple Logos

†"What meaning was originally conveyed by the world-wide symbol of the cross? Part, at any rate, of the answer is given to us by Madame Blavatsky herself in the proem to **The Secret Doctrine** when she describes the signs impressed upon the successive leaves of a certain archaic manuscript. It will be remembered that first of all there is the plain white circle which is understood to typify the Absolute; in that appears the central spot, the sign that the First Logos has entered upon a cycle of activity; the spot broadens into a line dividing the circle into two parts, thus symbolizing the dual aspect of the Second Logos as male-female, God-man, spirit-matter; and then, to show the next stage, this dividing line is crossed by another, and we have the heiroglyph of the Third Logos—God the Holy Ghost, the Lord, the Life-giver.

*The Secret Doctrine, by H. P. Blavatsky. Vol. 1, p. 34.
†The Christian Creed, by C. W. Leadbeater, pp. 88-89.

"But all these symbols, be it noted, are still within the circle, and so are emblems of different stages in the unfolding of the Triple Logos—not as yet of His manifestation."

The Egyptian Tau Another interesting development of the cross within the circle is the Egyptian Tau. This symbol is described by Madame Blavatsky as follows:

*"The diameter, when found isolated in a circle, stands for female Nature; for the first ideal World, self-generated and self-impregnated by the universally diffused Spirit of Life—thus also referring to the primitive Root-Race. It becomes androgynous as the Races and all else on Earth develop into their physical forms, and the symbol is transformed into a circle with a diameter from which runs a vertical line, expressive of male and female, not separated as yet—the first and earliest Egyptian Tau; ⊖ after which it becomes +, or male female separated and fallen into generation."

The Svastika Still another is Thor's hammer or the svastika. In this symbol one must think of the cross as representing the divine Flame, and then imagine its rapid rotation. This rotation would naturally result in four tongues or ribbons of flame flowing out of each arm as the cross revolves. God is here represented as the central Fire of the universe; this is the divine Flame. Within the soul of every human being there is a divine spark, which will in turn become a flame, and then it is that man will realize he is at-one with this divine or central Fire.

*The Secret Doctrine, by H. P. Blavatsky, Vol. II, pp. 33-4.

The Greek Cross　We now come to that stage where the divine Life makes a "further descent," in other words, the infinite Mind brings into manifestation step by step and stage by stage His infinite idea, the spiritual universe including man. His life is radiated or poured forth in every direction. This creative force or energy breaks up the circle, and we have remaining only the Greek cross with its open arms.

The Maltese Cross　Another and even better form of expressing the radiation of the divine Energy throughout all space and on all planes is the Maltese cross.

The Rose-Cross　Occasionally the Greek cross has a circle in the centre, and this circle is "said to blossom forth." Here we have the gradual unfolding of the rose, which of course represents the manifestation of the infinite Mind. This not only refers to the universe or macrocosm, but also to man the microcosm. This rose in the centre of the cross is the well-known Rosicrucian symbol. A wreath of seven roses on the cross is also a Rosicrucian symbol.

The Cross a Key to Man's Evolution　Max Heindel, the author of **Rosicrucian Cosmo-Conception**, has given us the following lucid description of the cross:

*"Viewed in its fullness, this wonderful symbol contains the key to man's past evolution, his present constitution and future development together with the method of attainment. In that form where it is represented with a single rose in the center it symbolizes the spirit radiating from itself the four vehicles; the

*Max Heindel (The Rosicrucian Fellowship).

dense, vital and desire-bodies plus the mind, where the spirit has drawn into its instruments and become the indwelling human spirit. But there was a time when that condition did not obtain, a time when the three-fold spirit hovered above its vehicles and was unable to enter. Then the cross stood alone without the rose, symbolizing the condition which prevailed in the early third of Atlantis. There was even a time when the upper limb of the cross was lacking and man's constitution was represented by the Tau (T) that was in the Lemurian epoch when he had only the dense, vital and desire bodies but lacked the mind. Then the animal nature was paramount. Man followed desire without reserve. At a still earlier time he was also minus desire-body and possessed only of the dense and vital bodies. Then man-in-the-making was like the plants: chaste and devoid of desire. At that time his constitution could not have been represented by a cross. It was symbolized by a straight shaft, a pillar (I).

* * * "The roses upon the cross indicate the path of liberation.

.   .   .   .

"In time the present passionate mode of generation will be again superceded by a pure and more efficient method than the present, and that also is symbolized in the Rose-cross where the rose is placed in the center between the four arms. The long limb represents the body, the two horizontals, the two arms and the upper limb, the head. Then the rose is in place of the larynx."

The Ansated Cross *"The Egyptians symbolized Ankh 'life,' by the ansated cross, or ♀ which is only

*The Secret Doctrine, by Madame Blavatsky. Vol. II. p. 34.

another form of Venus (Isis), ♀, and meant, Esoterically, that mankind and all animal life had stepped out of the divine spiritual circle and had fallen into physical male and female generation. This sign, from the end of the Third Race, has the same phallic significance as the 'Tree of Life' in Eden."

The cross is also sometimes represented thus:

All Life Is One So long as man realizes that this life is all one and that all things are in turn manifestations or expressions of the one divine infinite Mind, all is well; but the moment he ceases to partake of the fruit of this "Tree of Life" and begins to pluck the fruit from the tree of the knowledge of good and evil, just at that moment do all his troubles begin; for he must suffer for this false belief or ignorance, paying the penalty through disease and death.

In the second chapter of Genesis it is recorded that in the day that man eats thereof he shall surely die.

Jesus "Hanged on a Tree" It is significant that in the Acts the cross is referred to as a tree.

*"The God of our fathers raised up Jesus, whom ye slew and hanged on a tree."

†"And we are witnesses of all things which he did both in the land of the Jews, and in Jerusalem; whom ye slew and hanged on a tree."

Every man must symbolically be hanged on this tree; he must in other words kill out this lower sensual Adam belief. As the inner spiritual self or rose unfolds, this old man is actually put off: material sense

*Acts. v:30.
†Acts. x:39.

is transmuted into spiritual sense, man is transformed
or unlifted into Spirit. To express this idea more
clearly we might say that ignorance is dissipated or
overcome by divine Wisdom through the unfolding of
the inner Christlike self.

Christ Crucified on Golgotha In considering the crucifixion as explained by the four evangelists, we find that Christ was crucified on Golgotha or the place of a skull. This symbolizes the death of the animal or Adam nature.

The Two Thieves On each side of Jesus hung a thief. This fact must not be ignored, for what is it that steals away man's spiritual birthright? Surely it is the belief in two powers—good and evil, Spirit and matter. This false belief or error comes like a thief in the night and steals away everything that is precious and lovely, making man a prey to sin, disease and death. These two thieves, or this belief in two opposing or warring powers, must die before man can ascend to that glorious state of consciousness where all is light, life and love.

The Carnal Mind Loth to Recognize the Christ It is stated, "And they that were crucified with him reviled him," and also, "They that passed by reviled him, wagging their heads." The carnal mind is loth to recognize this immaculate Christ idea. Evil continually cries out against the Truth; "What have we to do with thee, thou Son of the most high God?" But Jesus only pitied them, for he knew that evil is ignorance; and he, being possessed of this knowledge, said, "Father, forgive them; for they know not what they do."

Death Transmuted Into Life

Within the consciousness of the Christ was a stillness, a peace and a love which sustained him and lifted him above the raging carnal minds by whom he was surrounded. This peace of God passes all human understanding. It flowed like a river through Christ's consciousness and sustained him in this hour of need. When the women were weeping, he said, "Weep not for me." Death and the crucifixion of the carnal mind is in reality not a sad but a joyous occasion. What appears to be a tragedy is in one sense the exact opposite, for death is to be transmuted into life. And now behold! there is no death, since God is Life and this Life is omnipresent and omnipotent. Thus Jesus, recognizing this stupendous fact, could say even in this seemingly dark hour, "Weep not for me." Weeping may endure for a night, but joy cometh in the morning; and he during this hour of trial and suffering was able to rise above the darkness into the Light and glory of omnipotent Life.

Darkness from the Sixth to the Ninth Hour

We are told that there was darkness from the sixth to the ninth hour. Six is the number of "temptation, sin, toil and punishment of sin." The darkness disappeared at the ninth hour, for nine is the square of three, it is the divine or heavenly number, and is sometimes spoken of as "Symbolic of the heavenly host." There are nine orders of angels mentioned in the epistle to the Ephesians. Nine is also referred to as the number of "Love and Law" since *"love is the fulfilling of the law." Christ through divine Love and through acting in obedience to the law of Love was to lift himself from darkness into light—from six to nine.

*Romans. xiii:10.

Christ's Yoke is Easy This achievement can only be accomplished by each one of us through following Christ's example. He is truly our way-shower, and we should all thank God daily that we have had this straight and narrow road pointed out to us. Some might conclude that a sad, toilsome and painful journey stretches before us, but when we realize that Christ's yoke is easy, we need have no fear. The inner, spiritual joys far outweigh the seeming suffering. We must remember that the suffering ceases the moment we relinquish the belief in any power opposed to Good. It is really extraordinary how the carnal mind clings to the lie that there are two powers.

What the Five Wounds Typify We shall now try to ascertain what the five wounds typify. The fact that Christ's hands, feet and heart were pierced is more than significant: man's fivefold material sense nature must be pierced for it is the limited carnal sense of life that holds man in bondage. The five senses are sometimes spoken of as the "five fetters" which bind earthly material man, and it is essential that man should rise to a point where these senses no longer fetter or control him. Christ was nailed to the cross of matter, but after receiving the fifth wound he was taken down from the cross.

The fifth wound was received in the heart—the seat of material life. Speaking allegorically we usually refer to the heart as the centre of the affections, and one often hears the expressions, good-hearted, warm-hearted, cold-hearted, and the like.

It is not easy, from a material point of view, to

The Cry of Agony at the Darkest Hour Before the Dawn rise to such a sublime height. The initiate cries out in agony when he reaches this stage in his spiritual development. It is recorded that Jesus cried with a loud voice: "My God, my God, why hast thou forsaken me?" This cry was uttered at the ninth hour—the darkest hour just before dawn—but light was soon to break in upon his consciousness: Jesus again cried with a loud voice and yielded up the ghost. This yielding up the ghost is really the giving up of all material sense of life. Jesus is now prepared to pass from death into life. We should constantly remind ourselves that nothing can possibly die except error, and that the beliefs now cast out and destroyed are false beliefs.

The Veil Rent in Twain We are told that at the moment Jesus gave up the ghost the veil of the temple was rent in twain from the top to the bottom; that there was a great earthquake, and also that the rocks were rent. When man has reached this stage, the veil of matter can no longer cloud his vision; he has reached that point where he sees spiritually, not materially. This veil is the limitation of the material senses. In our present state of consciousness we are like men groping about in a fog; nothing seems clear, there is a mist rising from the earth continually; nothing but the Sun of Righteousness can dissipate this cloud of matter. **Material Theories Quake in Truth's Presence** All material theories quake in the presence of Truth, all the time honoured hypotheses and so-called laws, if founded upon the supposition that there are two powers, must be rent in twain even though they seem to have a solid foundation. This material rock must give place to the rock Christ Jesus, that great corner stone in the temple of God. No so-called material power can withstand omnipotent Love. Even the Roman centurion was compelled to say: *"Truly this was the Son of God."

Christ's Garments Divided Into Four Parts In the Fourth Gospel we are told that when the soldiers had crucified Jesus they took his garments and divided them into four parts, giving a part to every soldier. These four parts represent the material garment or body that is to be put off with its deeds—four representing the world, matter and the lower nature. In **The Seamless Robe** addition to the garments which can be divided into four parts, there is also a coat †"without seam, woven from the top throughout." This garment, because it is one, or seamless, cannot be divided. "They said therefore among themselves, Let us not rend it, but cast lots for it." The one undivided garment symbolizes the spiritual body, which can neither be rent nor destroyed.

"It is Finished" It is recorded that after Jesus had received the vinegar, he cried out, "It is finished," and gave up the ghost. St. John tells us that the Jews, in order that the bodies of the crucified should not remain upon the cross on the Sabbath day begged Pilate that their legs might be broken, and that they might be taken away. The soldiers, after **Not a Bone Broken** breaking the legs of the two thieves, came to Jesus; but when they "saw that he was

*St. Matthew, xxvii:54.
†St. John, xix:23, 24.

dead already, they brake not his legs." The Scriptures
were therefore fulfilled that not a bone of his body
should be broken. Nothing that is really good can be
marred or destroyed.

Christ was to conquer death through rising above
the beliefs in sin, matter and the grave. There was to
be no body left in the tomb, he was to prove that all
is Spirit, and the manifestation of Spirit. There is but
one Life because God is one, and the whole universe,
including man, lives in this infinite ocean of divine
Energy.

The Heart   When one of the soldiers pierced the
Pierced   heart of Christ with a spear, "forthwith
came there out blood and water." This blood and
water is the divine Life, Christ-life; and in the various
myths and legends concerning the quest of the Holy
Grail, reference is made to Joseph of Arimathæa who
is supposed to have caught the blood in a cup so that
none should be spilled. Nothing connected with the
Christ-life can be lost. In Life (God) there is no death.

The Quest   "The story of the Grail" as related by
of the   Gurnemanz is as follows:
Holy Grail
             *"Four of the young squires crowd
around Gurnemanz and ask him to tell them the story
of the Grail and of Amfortas' wound. They all recline
beneath the tree, and Gurnemanz begins:

" 'On the night when our Lord and Savior Christ-
Jesus ate the last supper with his disciples he drank
the wine from a certain chalice and that was later
used by Joseph of Arithmathea to catch the life-blood

*Rosicrucian Christianity Series, Parsifal, by Max Heindel, pp. 6-7.

which flowed from the wound in the Redeemer's side.
He also kept the bloody lance wherewith the wound
was inflicted, and carried these relics with him through
many perils and persecutions. At last they were taken
in charge by angels, who guarded them until one night
a mystic messenger sent from God appeared and bade
Titurel, Amfortas' father, build a Castle for the recep-
tion and safe keeping of these relics. Thus the Castle
of Montsalvat was built on a high mountain, and the
relics lodged there under the guardianship of Titurel
with a band of holy and chaste knights whom he had
drawn around him, and it became a center whence
mighty spiritual influences went forth to the outside
world.'"

Joseph of Arimathæa Joseph of Arimathæa might be likened to
the mind, and this mind which is first
enslaved in Egypt has become more and more enlightened until there is no longer within it any belief in
matter. The lower carnal mind must eventually be
transmuted or lifted into a higher state of consciousness—the one Mind. The blood and water which at
first seem to be in matter will at last be found in God,
and from God, Who is Spirit. The blood must be lifted
up in a cup and carried by the angels to the haven
which is within us all. The quest of the Holy Grail is
The Christian Knight Who Treads "the Path" truly the quest of all quests. Each man
who treads "the path" is truly a Christian
knight; and he must be tested and tried,
for only thus can he be purified. He may
have many battles to fight, but he is sure to be victorious in the end if he follows his captain, Christ; not

one bone of his body will be broken, and though he may seem to lose his life, nevertheless not one drop of his blood will be spilled—all will be caught in the cup. The carnal mind which is at enmity with God is no mind, since it is ignorance. This so-called mind which is darkness will be found to be nothingness, since it becomes dissipated by the unfolding of the inner spiritual self. This spiritual self casts it off, as a snake casts its skin, or a crab its shell.

The Story of Kundry   The story of Kundry, a character in Parsifal, throws some light on the lower nature with its physical body, which is to be cast aside, crucified or transformed.

*"In Kundry we see a creature of two existences, one as servitor of the Grail, willing and anxious to further the interests of the Grail-knights by all means within her power; this seems to be her real nature. In the other existence she is the unwilling slave of the magician Klingsor and is forced by him to tempt and harass the Grail-knights, whom she longs to serve. The gate from one existence to the other is 'sleep,' and she is bound to serve who finds and wakes her. When Gurnemanz finds her she is the willing servitor of the Grail, but when Klingsor evokes her by his evil spells he is entitled to her services whether she will or not.

"In the first act she is clothed in a robe of snake skins, symbolical of the doctrine of re-birth, for as the snake sheds its skin, coat after coat, which it exudes from itself, so the Ego in its evolutionary pilgrimage emanates from itself one body after another, shedding

*Rosicrucian Christianity Series, Parsifal, by Max Heindel, pp. 5-6.

each vehicle as the snake sheds its skin, when it has become hard, set and crystallized so that it has lost its efficiency. This idea is also coupled with the teachings of the Law of Consequence, which brings to us as reapings whatever we sow."

The Old Adam Vanquished Anna Kingsford gives us the following lucid description of the crucifixion of the lower self:

*"And the particular act whereby this surrender is consummated and demonstrated, is called the Crucifixion. This crucifixion means a complete, unreserving surrender,—to the death, if need be,— without opposition, even in desire, on the part of the natural man. Without these steps is no atonement. The man cannot become one with the spirit within him, until by his 'Passion' and 'Crucifixion,' he has utterly vanquished the 'old Adam' of his former self."

Bound to the Cross of Matter Mr. C. W. Leadbeater explains, in the following paragraph, how we are bound to the cross of matter:

†"It may serve to remind us also that man himself is thus crucified, if he did but know it; and that if he knows it not, it is because the living soul, the true Christ within him, is still blindly identifying himself with the cross of matter to which he is bound. It may help us to realize that our bodies, whether physical, astral or mental, are not ourselves, and that whenever we find, as it were, two selves warring within us, we have to remember that we are in truth the higher, and not the lower—the Christ, and not the cross."

*The Perfect Way, by Anna Kingsford M. D., p. 213.
†The Christian Creed, by C. W. Leadbeater, pp. 96-97.

Matter to be Ingested or Indrawn   *"In regard to this aspect of the Christ the recovered Gnosis discourses as follows:—

" 'There is a power by means of which matter may be ingested into its original substance.

" 'He who possesses this power is Christ, and he has the devil under foot.

" 'For he reduces chaos to order, and indraws the external to the centre.

Matter is Illusion   " 'He has learnt that matter is illusion, and that spirit alone is real.

Spirit is Real.   " 'He has found his own central point: and all power is given unto him in heaven and on earth. * * *

" 'Not that matter shall be destroyed, * * * but it shall be indrawn and resolved into its true self. * * *

" 'The body, which is matter, is but the manifestation of spirit: and the Word of God shall transmute it into its inner being."

The Gnostic Crucifixion   The following excerpt from **The Gnostic Crucifixion** is intensely interesting, and throws much light on the crucifixion:—

†"And when He was hung on the tree of the cross, at the sixth hour of the day darkness came over the whole earth.

"And my Lord stood in the midst of the Cave, and and filled it with light, and said:

" 'John, to the multitude below, in Jerusalem, I am

---

*The Bible's Own Account of Itself, by Edward Maitland, p. 48.
†Echoes from the Gnosis—The Gnostic Crucifixion—The Vision of the Cross—by G. R. S. Mead. 3, 4, 5, 6, 14, 24, 25, pp. 13-15, 18, 19.

being crucified, and pierced with spears and reeds, and vinegar and gall is being given Me to drink. * * *'

"And having thus spoken, He showed me a Cross of Light set up, and round the Cross a vast multitude. * * *

" 'This Cross of Light is called by Me for your sakes sometimes Word (Logos), sometimes Mind, sometimes Jesus, sometimes Christ, sometimes Door, sometimes Way. * * *

.   .   .   .

" 'Now the multitude of one appearance round the Cross is the Lower Nature.' * * *

.   .   .   .

"And having said these things to me, and others which I know not how to say as He Himself would have it, He was taken up, no one of the multitude beholding Him.

"And when I descended I laughed at them all, when they told Me what they did concerning Him, firmly possessed in myself of this [truth] only, that the Lord contrived all things **symbolically,** and according to [His] dispensation for the conversion and salvation of man."

Mr. Mead, in his comments on **The Vision of the Cross,** writes:—

The Mount of Olives and Jerusalem Defined *"But to the Gnostic the Mount of Olives was no physical hill, though it was a mount in the physical, and Jerusalem no physical city, though a city in the physical. The Mount, however it might be distinguished locally, was the Height of Contemplation, and the

*Echoes from the Gnosis—The Gnostic Crucifixion. pp. 22-24.

bringing into activity of a certain inner consciousness; even as Jerusalem here was the Jerusalem below, the physical consciousness.

The Tree of Fiery Life " * * * The Tree of Fiery Life, in the Paradise of man's inner nature, where the Word of God expresses itself to one who is worthy to hear. And this Tree of Life was also, as the Cross, the Tree of Knowledge of Good and Evil."

Christ's Burial Christ was buried in a new tomb hewn out of the solid rock, and in front of this tomb was rolled a great stone. There was also a guard of Roman soldiers. The scribes and Pharisees had come to Pilate, saying, *"Sir, we remember that that deceiver said, while he was yet alive, After three days I will rise again." And they had begged for the sepulchre to be made sure; they were afraid that the disciples would come by night and steal the body. But all precautions taken by the mortal mind are useless.

The Stone of Matter Rolled Back Christ overcomes error. There was a great earthquake, and the angel of the Lord descends and rolls back the stone of matter. No wonder the keepers shake and become as dead men, for his countenance is like lightning and his raiment white as snow. The carnal mind is persistent to the end; always doubting, always afraid, it is †"good for nothing, but to be cast out and to be trodden under foot of men." It is salt that has lost its "savour."

The stone was rolled away at dawn. Behold the night is past, and light breaks in upon the conscious-

*St. Matthew, xxvii:63.
†St. Matthew, v:13.

ness, dissipating all error, just as material light neutralizes or dissipates darkness. This resurrection is truly
transmutation; all the dross is now burnt away leaving
man's nature pure gold.

Resurrection, *"For there is nothing which can go out
Trans- from the presence of God.
figuration,
Transmu- "This is the doctrine of the resurrection
tation of the dead: that is, the transfiguration of
the body.

"For the body, which is matter, is but the manifestation of spirit: and the Word of God shall transmute it
into its inner being.

"The will of God is the alchemic crucible: and the
dross that is cast therein is matter.

"And the dross shall become pure gold, seven times
refined; even perfect spirit."

Jesus' Third The last incident to be mentioned in this
Appearance chapter is Jesus' third appearance to his
to His disciples at the Sea of Tiberias. †"Simon
Disciples Peter, and Thomas called Didymus, and
Nathanael of Cana in Galilee, and the sons of Zebedee,
and two other of his disciples" had been fishing all
night and had caught nothing. As the morning was
breaking Jesus was seen standing on the shore, but the
disciples were not aware that it was he. He said unto
them: "Children, have ye any meat? They answered
him, No." Jesus then commanded them to cast their
"net on the right side of the ship." They obeyed and
behold their net was full. They "drew the net to land
full of great fishes, an hundred and fifty and three: and
for all there were so many, yet was not the net broken."

*"Clothed with the Sun." by Anna Kingsford. M. D., p. 236.

As soon as the disciples reached land "they saw a fire of coals there, and fish laid thereon, and bread." Jesus requested that they should bring of the fish that they had caught, and then gave them bread "and fish likewise."

Fishing in the Shallows of Matter There are many lessons to be learnt from this incident. First it should be noted that the disciples were fishing in the night and on the wrong side of the ship. All night they had toiled and caught nothing: it was only when they cast their net on the right side that 153 fish were secured.

So long as we are in the darkness of materialism, fishing in the shallows of matter and the carnal mind, just so long shall we be disappointed, for sorrow, heartache, sickness and death follow such misdirected actions. It is only when the light breaks in on the consciousness—when the Christ appears on the shore in the morning—that we realize how foolish it is to search for satisfaction in matter. It is only when we fish in the depths of Spirit that we are rewarded.

The Fish The fish is a most interesting symbol. Jesus said, in speaking of gifts, *"If he (a son) ask a fish, will he (the father) give him a serpent?" It will also be remembered that Jesus paid tribute money from coin taken from a fish's mouth, and that he fed the five thousand with fish and bread.

The Mahabharata Story of the Deluge and the Fish The fish was an emblem used among the early Christians, but it antedates Christianity, for we read in The Mahabharata, in the story of the deluge of how a fish †"towed the ark with great force through

*St. Matthews, vii:10.
†The Mahabharata, Vol. II. p. 555.

the salt waters. And it conveyed them in that vessel on the roaring and billow-beaten sea." And although "the vessel reeled about like a drunken harlot, * * * the fish diligently dragged the boat through the flood for many a long year. * * * It towed the vessel toward the highest peak of the Himavat. And O Bhārat, the fish then told those on the vessel to tie it to that peak of the Himavat. And hearing the words of the fish, they immediately tied the boat on that peak of the mountain." The fish then addresses the inhabitants of the boat in the following words: "I am Brahmā, the Lord of all creatures; there is none greater than myself. Assuming the shape of a fish, I have saved ye from this cataclysm. * * * By practising severe austerities, he (Manu) will acquire this power, and with my blessing, illusion will have no power over him."

The Lord Saves Man from Illusion   This passage gives us the true meaning of the word "fish," for nothing but "the Lord of all creatures" can save man from the illusion of the material senses—the belief in a power opposed to Good—and guide him over this tempestuous sea of life to the haven of Spirit, where there is neither sorrow nor crying nor any more pain.

The Words "Deluge" and "Water" Contrasted   The reader should note the difference in meaning between the words "deluge" and "water." The former stands ,symbolically, for "Chaotic unsettled Matter," while the meaning of the latter is "the Feminine Principle—the 'Great Deep.'"

Jesus Christ
Our Saviour
The Greek word for fish is ΙΧΘΥΣ, and this forms the initials of the following Greek words, the translation of which is "Jesus Christ of God, the Son (our) Saviour."

Ιησοῦς
Χριςτος
Θεοῦ
Υιος
Σωτήρ

From the above it will be observed how beautifully this definition agrees with the passage quoted from the Mahabharata.

Little Fishes
Saved by One
Great Fish
*"St. Augustin says of Jesus: 'He is a fish that lives in the midst of waters.' Christians called themselves 'Little Fishes'—Pisciculi—in their sacred Mysteries. 'So many fishes bred in the water, and **saved by one great fish**,' says Tertullian of the Christians and Christ and the Church."

The Carved
Stone at
Tintern
Abbey
The reproduction on the opposite page was made from a rough sketch of a cross, which was originally carved on a large slab of stone. This stone is still in a perfect state of preservation, and can be seen within the ruined walls of Tintern Abbey.

The Inner
Meaning
of 153
It might be asked why there were 153 fish in the net. The number is explained in this way. Seven is the perfect spiritual man, while ten stands for the Law or divine Principle. 10+7=17, or the "fulfillment of the Law by the works

*The Secret Doctrine, by H. P. Blavatsky, Vol. II, p. 327.

Carved Stone at Tintern Abbey, Monmouthshire,
England.

of the Spirit." We are told that faith without works is dead, and that we must work out our own salvation. This can only be accomplished step by step, for it is a long journey. One must follow in the footsteps of the Christ. One might say that this fulfillment of the Law by the works of the Spirit, and the steps leading thereto is symbolized by the progression:

*1+2+3+4 . . . +16 17=153.

Spirit, Not Matter, Saves We thus see how the Law is fulfilled and by what means the blood (or life) of Jesus Christ cleanses from all sin: Spirit, not matter, saves: divine Principle or Law, not the so-called laws of the carnal mind, must be obeyed if the initiate is ever to become a king and priest unto God. "The law of the spirit of life in Christ Jesus" frees man absolutely from "the law of sin and death."

All that is Good Must be Saved The 153 fish in the net also symbolizes "the blessed company of all faithful people." All that is good must be saved since that which is spiritual cannot be destroyed. One can now readily see why Christ fed the disciples on fish and bread, and also why the fish was roasted, for the fire symbolizes the divine Fire.

The Hungry Multitude The hungry multitude of five thousand people were also fed on fish and bread, for fish and bread alone can satisfy the hungry soul. And if we ask the Father for fish He will not give us a serpent: neither will He give us a stone when we ask for bread. It is only out of the fish's mouth that the money can be taken, for Spirit, not matter, is Sub-

*Chapters on Symbolism, by W. Frank Shaw, p. 126.

stance and supplies all our needs. A man may gain
Material the whole world and yet lose his own soul.
Riches Material riches never satisfy; it is the
Never Satisfy spiritual riches, the pearls of great price
that satisfy the soul. Blessed is the man to whom
Christ appears; and when the command is given him
to cast his net out of matter into Spirit, he is wise if he
immediately obeys, for he will be rewarded: his net
will be full, and his cup will run over with peace and
joy and an abundance of good things from the Father's
table.

The journey is long and the way is narrow, but it
leads straight to the goal, and the goal is sure.

Ascending The beautiful spiral stairway which man
Life's Spiral is ascending, and the temple of God which
Stairway he is building is referred to by Oliver
Wendell Holmes in the following inspiring stanzas:

"Year after year behold the silent toil
That spreads his lustrous coil;
Still, as the spiral grew,
He left the past year's dwelling for the new,
Stole with soft step its shining archway through,
Built up its idle door,
Stretched in his last-found home, and knew the old no more.

"Thanks for the heavenly message brought by thee,
Child of the wandering sea,
Cast from her lap forlorn!
From thy dead lips a clearer note is borne
Than ever Triton blew from wreathed horn!
While on mine ear it rings,
Through the deep caves of thought I hear a voice that sings:

"Build thee more stately mansions, O my soul!
As the swift seasons roll!
Leave thy low-vaulted past!
Let each new temple, nobler than the last,
Shut thee from heaven with a dome more vast,
Till thou at length art free,
Leaving thine outgrown shell by life's unresting sea!"

CHAPTER VI.

"THESE SIGNS SHALL FOLLOW THEM THAT BELIEVE"

The world is full of heartache and misery; on every hand we see sin, disease and death; and the man who relies solely on the testimony of the material senses must inevitably become a pessimist, an iconoclast.

Mental Renewal Followed by Bodily Transformation But above and beyond and within all discord is the soul, the real self, the image and likeness of God, the real or spiritual man who is subject to neither time nor space, who is never born and never dies, and who has his being in Spirit. This is the Christ man, and it is the unfolding of the inner self that lifts man above sin and misery and heals him spiritually, mentally, morally and physically. It is, as St. Paul expresses it, this mental renewal which brings about a transformation of the physical body. Christ's mission was not only to forgive sins but to heal the sick, and if the Scriptures are to be believed, healing was one of the most important parts of his mission on earth.

Christ's Last Message There is one way in which truth can be proved to be truth by mortals, and that is by demonstration. Jesus made it quite clear that certain signs were to follow those who believed; we were not to be left comfortless. The last message of the Christ to his disciples, is most significant. When a man starts on a long journey, he often leaves his most important wishes or instructions until the last moment. We should therefore follow carefully this final message of Jesus:

*"Go ye into all the world, and preach the gospel to every creature.

.   .   .   .

"And these signs shall follow them that believe; In my name shall they cast out devils; they shall speak with new tongues;

"They shall take up serpents; and if they drink any deadly thing, it shall not hurt them; they shall lay hands on the sick, and they shall recover."

Nothing could be plainer than this command. The test then as to whether we really know the truth is this: are there any signs following? If not, there must be something awry with our understanding of the truth.

Biblical Authority for Spiritual Healing Will anyone have the temerity to assert that a man who has never worked out a problem is a mathematician? The same rule evidently holds good with Christianity, if Christ's words are to be taken seriously. And that they are to be taken seriously we who believe in the Bible know, for from one end of the Bible to the other we have authority for spiritual healing.

*St. Mark. xvi:15. 17. 18.

In the Garden of Eden God promised that the seed of the woman should bruise the serpent's head.

While the children of Israel were in the wilderness the Lord said:

God Heals the Sick *"If thou wilt diligently hearken to the voice of the Lord thy God, and wilt do that which is right in his sight, and wilt give ear to his commandments, and keep all his statutes, I will put none of these diseases upon thee, which I have brought upon the Egyptians: for I am the Lord that healeth thee."

The following message was sent to King Hezekiah:

God Hears and Answers Prayer †"Turn again, and tell Hezekiah the captain of my people, Thus saith the Lord, the God of David thy father, I have heard thy prayer, I have seen thy tears: behold, I will heal thee."

In the Psalms we have many beautiful promises with regard to healing, and the three following quotations are particularly encouraging and comforting:

The Sinner, the Heart-Broken and the Diseased Healed ‡"He healeth the broken in heart, and bindeth up their wounds."
||"Who forgiveth all thine iniquities; who healeth all thy diseases."
§"He sent his word, and healed them, and delivered them from their destructions."

*Exodus. xv:26.
†II Kings. xx:5.
‡Psalms. cxlvii:3.

||Psalms. ciii:3.
§Psalms. cvii:20.

The prophets also echo this healing message:

Isaiah and Ezekiel Echo the Healing Message *"Then shall thy light break forth as the morning, and thine health shall spring forth speedily: and thy righteousness shall go before thee; the glory of the Lord shall be thy reward." †"And it shall come to pass, that everything that liveth, which moveth, whithersoever the rivers shall come, shall live: and there shall be a very great multitude of fish, because these waters shall come thither: for they shall be healed; and every thing shall live whither the riveth cometh."

Bearing in mind the symbolical meaning of the fish, this quotation is intensely interesting.

Solomon tells us:

Solomon's Testimony ‡"The tongue of the wise is health."

St. John's Statement The following passage from the third epistle of St. John seems to indicate that we should prosper and be in good physical health when we are spiritually healthy:

‖"Beloved, I wish above all things that thou mayest prosper and be in health, even as thy soul prospereth."

Christ Heals the Sick Practically the whole of Christ's public life was spent in healing the sick. To

*Isaiah, lviii:8.
†Ezekiel, xlvii:9.
‡Proverbs, xii:18.
‖III John, verse 2.

eliminate this portion of his ministry would be utterly impossible since it was the proof to the unbelieving that he was one with his Father, and that he came to this world with divine authority. Behind his works was omnipotent, divine, ever-present Love. He knew that of himself he could do nothing, but that through and by the power of God the whole world was at his feet.

Palsy Healed   Much can be learnt from the careful study of some of the most important of Christ's miracles. Take, for example, the healing of the man suffering with palsy mentioned in the fifth chapter of St. Luke's Gospel. It is recorded that there was a great multitude of people surrounding Jesus at the time, and so great was the press it was impossible to reach him. The friends of the sick man therefore let him down through the roof in his bed to the feet of the Master. When Jesus saw their faith, he immediately said, "Man, thy sins are forgiven thee."

The scribes and Pharisees took exception to these words, and looked upon Jesus as a blasphemer, for they said, "Who can forgive sins, but God alone?"

Truth Destroys Both Sin and Disease   Jesus perceived their thoughts, and the question with which he confronted them, was far-reaching in its significance: "Whether is easier, to say, Thy sins be forgiven thee; or to say, Rise up and walk?" He then commanded the man to rise, take up his bed and walk. And the man immediately arose, "and took up that whereon he lay, and departed to his own house, glorifying God."

Spiritual Healing is not Suggestion It is often dogmatically asserted by latter-day critics that spiritual healing is nothing more than suggestion. Nothing could be wider of the mark. Between suggestion and spiritual healing a great gulf is fixed. The carnal mind continually endeavors to ape the stately and ordered action of the divine Mind, and evil ever masquerades in the stolen or counterfeit vestments of Truth; but the carnal mind must give place to divine understanding.

Ascertain and Destroy the Cause of a Disease When a man is ill, to simply suggest that he is well is worse than foolishness; in fact, it is both pernicious and dangerous. To remove an effect blindly without ascertaining the cause is like firemen directing their efforts to the smoke without discovering the seat of the fire. Disease is an effect, and one might confidently assert that the cause of all disease and misery in the world is either ignorance or sin. Broadly speaking, it is ignorance of Good, or want of knowledge of the divine Law.

Jesus Struck at the Root of the Disease It was not the aim of Jesus merely to remove effects: in no sense was his work superficial. He struck at the root of the disease, for he well knew that the only way radically and permanently to exterminate it was to destroy the sin or error of which this disease was a manifestation or expression. The Pharisees were astonished at his audacity, yea, blasphemy, in presuming to be possessed of this power; but we know that "Christ is the divine manifestation of God," and that therefore his words, "Thy sins are forgiven thee," are neither presumptuous nor blasphemous.

The Inexhaustible Healing Stream

Jesus said on one occasion, *"The words that I speak unto you, they are spirit, and they are life." Jesus the Christ, being at-one with his Father, was a channel through which this divine Life was ever flowing like a river. It was a pure, clear, inexhaustible stream, welling up within him. And this same well of water is within the soul of every human being, although it may not as yet have been discovered. It is often necessary to bore to a considerable depth before man becomes aware of its presence, for it lies deep beneath

Greater Works Shall Ye Do

the error that has been accumulating for ages. Jesus said, †"Verily, verily, I say unto you, He that believeth on me, the works that I do shall he do also; and greater works than these shall he do; because I go unto my Father." This promise should continually encourage us and urge us forward to renewed efforts, although the way at present may seem dark and gloomy.

St. Paul's Thorn in the Flesh

But the critic may ask what authority we have for assuming that all disease and suffering are the result of sin and ignorance. He points out that some of the best people in the world suffer, and reminds us that even St. Paul suffered from a thorn in the flesh, and that though he prayed to have it removed, he prayed without avail, the Lord replying, ‡"My grace is sufficient for thee: for my strength is made perfect in weakness."

Spiritual Strength

Now, "my strength is made perfect in weakness" does not mean that a Christian

*St. John, vi:63.
†St. John, xiv:12.
‡II Corinthians, xii:9.

to be a Christian must be a weak man. On the contrary he is spiritually a strong man; and Jesus the Christ, our way-shower, was the strongest man who ever lived. He was also the essence of gentleness, and his nature was like that of a little child. His love was unchanging, and his patience inexhaustible.

In such spiritual strength the worldly-minded sees only weakness, failing to understand that in the human will there is no real power, but spiritual strength exists independently of mere animality or physique: and the size of a man's muscles will give you no clue to his spirituality or his moral strength and courage.

A Perfect Mind in a Perfect Body Nevertheless, one should not jump to the conclusion that spirituality is necessarily accompanied by physical weakness. There is no reason why moral strength should not be accompanied by physical strength. Surely the ideal state is a perfect mind in a perfect body. If Jesus was ever physically ill the Scriptures do not record the fact.

It may be necessary for man to experience suffering before he is able to realize the inner meaning of life, but to stop short at the point of suffering is to misinterpret the significance of pain. Thank God, there is a stage above pain and misery, where peace, joy and health are divinely natural.

The "Thorn" is Useful in Teaching a Lesson St. Paul's statement, *"Most gladly therefore will I rather glory in my infirmities, that the power of Christ may rest upon me" must not be misinterpreted. He confesses that there was a danger of his being †"exalted

*II Corinthians, xii:9.
†Ibid, verse 7.

above measure." Therefore the "thorn" was evidently useful in teaching him a lesson at this particular stage of his spiritual development. Do not forget that the thorn was in the flesh, and that it was the messenger of Satan, not God. And if St. Paul had possessed more grace, if he had, in other words, been blessed with an understanding equal to that of the Christ, he would have given the same reply that the Christ gave:

*"Get thee behind me, Satan: for it is written, Thou shalt worship the Lord thy God, and him only shalt thou serve.   *   *   *

"Thou shalt not tempt the Lord thy God." And thus his thorn would have disappeared.

Every Thirsty Soul May Drink The student should make a careful study of the 55th chapter of Isaiah. Here every thirsty soul is invited to drink of the spiritual healing waters. We can both eat and drink of this spiritual repast "without money and without price."

We read:

"Eat ye that which is good, and let your soul delight itself in fatness."

There is no threat of suffering in this invitation; and while we are warned that the wicked must forsake his sin, we are told that God "will have mercy" and that "he will abundantly pardon."

Suffering Follows Sin It is clear then that so long as we sin we must suffer. Why we suffer is made clear in the eighth verse: our thoughts and ways, owing to

*St. Luke, iv:8, 12.

our ignorance and undeveloped state, are not God's thoughts and God's ways.

Jesus came to show us the way and to teach us how to think; and just to the extent that we follow his instructions shall we be free from suffering and from the limitations of this world.

God's word will not return unto Him void, but it shall prosper in the thing whereto He sent it. And we shall go out with joy and be led forth with peace.

The Thorn Removed In the last verse of this beautiful chapter we read that the firtree will displace the thorn. So the thorn in man's flesh will give place to health. Satan will have no more power to buffet us when we know that he is a liar, and impotent in the presence of omnipotent Good.

Suffering undoubtedly is beneficial up to a certain stage of man's development, for it serves as a pin prick or reminder that he has broken the law of God, that he is ignorant, and furthermore that he must bring himself into unity with "the law of the spirit of life in Christ Jesus" which frees him eternally from bondage, sin, suffering and death.

Two Paths But Christ came to point out that the path of suffering is to be superseded by the path of science or knowledge of the Truth. To bear pain with patience and fortitude is commendable up to a point, and it is certainly preferable to cursing God. But surely the higher way is to pray for understanding whereby the sin or error may be uncovered and destroyed: the sin or error being thus removed, the effect must also disappear. The suffering of many saintly souls would be overcome if they fully understood this most important phase of Christ's teaching.

To be physically healed without being spiritually regenerated and transformed would do a man more harm than good. The healing of disease, then, is the natural outcome of the healing of sin. Jesus, in answering the scribes and Pharisees, made it quite clear that he had come, not to call the righteous, but sinners to repentance.

Seek First the Kingdom of Heaven Suggestion can never heal the sin-sick soul. Nothing but the power of God can lift a man above the sorrows of earth into the joys of heaven, and we are distinctly told that if a man seeks first the kingdom of heaven, all other things will be added unto him.

The *"prayer of faith," says St. James, "shall save the sick, and the Lord shall raise him up," but he also says: "If he have committed sins, they shall be forgiven him." We are further commanded to confess our "faults one to another, and pray one for another" that we may be healed.

Effectual Fervent Prayer It is "the effectual fervent prayer of a righteous man (that) availeth much," while it is quite possible for a man who is an atheist or an agnostic or even a scoffer at things religious, to use suggestion. Can it be said, then, that there is anything in suggestion akin to spiritual healing?

Magic and Necromancy In the Old Testament we read that the prophets of Baal tried to imitate the won-

*James. v:15, 16.

ders performed by the true prophets of God. The magicians, soothsayers and necromancers of Assyria, Chaldea and Babylonia also tried to imitate the wonders wrought by the spiritually minded, but they failed ignominiously. The wonders wrought by the carnal mind inevitably come to nought since they have no principle to govern them. Unless we build on the rock Christ Jesus, all our works are useless; we must have that mind in us which was also in Christ Jesus; it is only then that our prayers will be effectual.

Man the Mouthpiece for God   The scribes and Pharisees were right when they asserted that God alone could forgive sins. It is a blessed, encouraging and inspiring thought, however, to realize that man can actually be the mouthpiece for God, and that through his prayers or declaration of Truth he can so uplift a suffering mortal as to bring him into unity with this great healing power.

*"But the natural man receiveth not the things of the Spirit of God: for they are foolishness unto him: neither can he know them, because they are spiritually discerned."

Spiritual Discernment   The materialist often finds it difficult to distinguish between spiritual healing and material healing or suggestion, for the simple reason that he has never experienced that illumination, that new birth to which reference has already been made. In order that we may comprehend the mysteries of the kingdom of God, it is essential that we should grow in spirituality, that our inner self should be unfolded,

*I Corinthians, ii:14.

that material sense should give place to spiritual sense, that our blind eyes should see the light; for only thus is it possible for man to understand Christ's teaching and the mysteries connected with spiritual healing. A man looking through red glasses sees everything tinged with red: the materialist, if he would see truly, must cast aside his materialistic glasses; if he does not, he will continually fall into errors of judgment.

Did Jesus Use Material Means? Many storms of controversy have raged around the ninth chapter of the gospel of St. John. Christians who believe that material means are absolutely necessary point to this allegory in triumph; for here, they say, is an authentic instance of Christ using material means.

"He spat on the ground, and made clay of the spittle, and he anointed the eyes of the blind man with the clay.   .

The Blind Man Healed Jesus, it will be remembered, was passing by and saw a man who had been blind from his birth; and the disciples questioned him as to whether this man had sinned or his parents, since he had been born blind. The disciples evidently concluded that the blindness was the result of sin; and it might be mentioned here that on one occasion Jesus, after having healed a sufferer, said: *"Behold, thou art made whole: sin no more, lest a worse thing come unto thee," showing conclusively that the disease was the result of sin, and that to persist in this sin must result in dire suffering and catastrophy.

*St. John, v:14.

Jesus' Mystifying Answer Jesus' answer to his disciples is mystifying to the superficial thinker, and yet when examined closely is found to be full of meaning,

"Neither hath this man sinned, nor his parents: but that the works of God should be made manifest in him."

The Key to the Mystery Critics have frequently asserted that it is a cruel thing for a man who has not sinned to be born blind; and this problem like hundreds of others contained in the Bible can only be solved by probing beneath the surface. The key to this mystery is to be found in the last three verses of this same chapter where Jesus states that he came into the world **"that they which see not might see; and that they which see might be made blind."** The Pharisees upon hearing this assertion, asked, "Are we blind also?" And here follows a most important answer, every word of which must be noted: "Jesus said unto them, **If ye were blind, ye should have no sin: but now ye say, We see; therefore your sin remaineth."**

Blinded by Material Reason It is undoubtedly true that none are so blind as those who through ignorance, arrogance, pride, prejudice and pharisaism think they are wise. So long as a man is blinded by material reason and the material senses it is most difficult for him to see spiritually. It must therefore be true that it is only when a man realizes with humility and a childlike sense that the flesh profiteth nothing, and that the spiritual and not the material is the real, that he is ready to receive his spiritual sight. Jesus

A Pharisee Must Become Blind knew that these Pharisees must become blind before it was possible for them to see, and that they must understand that the knowledge of this world is to God very largely foolishness. The pharisaical self-righteous thought is one of the greatest barriers to spiritual progress and to the development of that inner intuitive sense that is so necessary to the man who is trying to follow in Christ's footsteps. So long then as the Pharisees arrogantly believed that they could see spiritually, just so long was their sin to remain.

We must all avoid this pharisaical blind thought, and we should, allegorically speaking, be born blind. It will now be seen that this blindness from birth has nothing to do with sin, but on the contrary is that state of mind, which when reached, makes it possible for the "works of God" to be "made manifest" in us.

The next point to be considered in this story is whether Christ used material means.

The Application of Clay In the sixth verse we read that he spat on the ground and, making clay of the spittle, anointed the eyes of the blind man. What could be plainer? says the materialist, for Christ actually restored this man's sight by the application of the clay.

Spitting a Sign of Contempt But the materialist must not be too hasty in drawing his conclusions. Among the Jews, spitting was the sign of utter contempt. It will be remembered that when the Jews wished to show their disrespect to the Christ they spat upon him. Jesus, on this occasion, wished to teach a spiritual lesson. "He spat on the ground, and made clay," spread it over the man's eyes and then commanded him to go and "wash in the pool of Siloam. * * * He went his way therefore, and washed, and came seeing." If it had been the intention of Jesus to use the clay medicinally he would not have instructed the blind man to go immediately and wash it off. But by the command he showed that it is not until the material sense of life is washed away by the water of Spirit that we gain the insight of the initiate.

The Pool of Siloam   Doctor Young tells us that the Pool of Siloah, or Siloam, is "at the king's gardens, south of Jerusalem;" and the word Siloam mentioned in this chapter is identical with Siloah referred to in Nehemiah: *"The pool of Siloah by the king's garden, and unto the stairs that go down from the city of David." The meaning of the word Siloah is "sending forth."

This kingly garden is really that state of consciousness, or shall we say that soul, wherein the Christ rules supreme: the literal meaning of the Greek word **Christos** being, as all know, **anointed.** The practice of anointing kings has been handed down for thousands of years, and King George was actually anointed with oil at his coronation.

In the centre of this divinely royal garden is the pool or well of water, and it is only when we go down to this pool and wash that we come up with our eyes open. We then see spiritually: the clay or materiality has been washed off by the water of Spirit, and we no longer "see through a glass darkly."

*Nehemiah. iii:15.

The Inner Meaning of Clay

The following passages will give the reader a clear conception of the inner meaning of the word clay.

*"He brought me up also out of an horrible pit, out of the miry clay, and set my feet upon a rock, and established my goings."

†"Thou, O king, sawest, and behold a great image. This great image, whose brightness was excellent, stood before thee; and the form thereof was terrible.

"This image's head was of fine gold, his breast and his arms of silver, his belly and his thighs of brass,

"His legs of iron, his feet part of iron and part of clay.

"Thou sawest till that a stone was cut out out without hands, which smote the image upon his feet that were of iron and clay, and brake them to pieces.

"Then was the iron, the clay, the brass, the silver, and the gold, broken to pieces together, and became like the chaff of the summer threshingfloors; and the wind carried them away, that no place was found for them: and the stone that smote the image became a great mountain, and filled the whole earth."

Upwelling of the Spiritual Water

If this explanation be correct, can we by any stretch of the imagination come to the conclusion that Christ really used material means in the healing of this

*Psalms, xl:2.
†Daniel, ii:31-35.

blind man. It was in reality the "sending forth," the upwelling of the spiritual water within this man's soul or consciousness, which washed or healed him. He was ready to be healed because he felt the need of spiritual sight, and it is those who hunger and thirst after righteousness that are rewarded. *"Desire is prayer:" it is necessary to desire God's blessings, and to desire them earnestly, before we are fit to receive them.

In the epistle of St. James we read:

Anointing With Oil "Is any sick among you? let him call for the elders of the church; and let them pray over him, anointing him with oil in the name of the Lord."

The critic might affirm that it was the oil in this case that healed the sick man, but the inspired writer informs us that it was the prayer of faith which saved the sick, and not the oil. The oil was merely symbolical of that kingly state of consciousness wherein and whereby man gains dominion over sin and disease. There is a very close connection between this oil with which the elders were to anoint a sick man and the pool in the king's garden.

Again we might turn to the 38th chapter of the book of Isaiah where we read that Hezekiah was sick unto death. In the 21st verse it is written:

A "Plaister" of Figs "Let them take a lump of figs, and lay it for a plaister upon the boil, and he shall recover."

*Science and Health, by Mary Baker Eddy, p. 1.

The superficial reader would naturally jump to the conclusion that it was the "plaister" made of figs which was responsible for the healing. However, we read that it was the love of God for Hezekiah's soul which "delivered it from the pit of corruption." Furthermore, Hezekiah's sins had been cast behind the Lord's back; in other words, his sins had been forsaken, forgiven and destroyed; and this forgiveness made it possible for him to be physically healed. In the 18th and 19th verses we read:

> "For the grave cannot praise thee, death can not celebrate thee: they that go down into the pit cannot hope for thy truth.
> "The living, the living, he shall praise thee, as I do this day."

This story of the recovery of Hezekiah is still more interesting when we study the symbolical meaning of the word fig.

Fig Defined   *"From time immemorial," says Edward Maitland, "the fig has been the mystical symbol for the soul as the feminine principle in man, having been selected to this end, because, while it is in the similitude of the ungravid matrix, it bears its blossoms interiorly, in darkness and concealment, as does the soul herself, and thus represents those truths which, being interior, mystic, spiritual, are discernible only by a special spirit of understanding."

The Fig-Branch   It is also well to remember that the fig-branch is the special symbol of Hermes, †"the 'angel of Understanding.' "

*"The Bible's Own Account of Itself, by Edward Maitland B. A., p. 63.
†Ibid.

The following lines also throw great light on the esoteric meaning of the fig:

*"Evoi, ('Hail') Iacchos: ('spiritual life') Lord of the body, and of the house whose symbol is the fig;

"Whereof the image is the figure of the matrix, and the leaf as a man's hand: whose stems bring forth milk.

"For the Woman is the mother of the living; and the crown and perfection of humanity.

"Her body is the highest step in the ladder of incarnation,

"Which leadeth from earth to Heaven; upon which the spirits of God ascend and descend.

The Soul Must Know Womanhood "Thou art not perfected, O soul, that hast not known womanhood.

"Evoi, Iacchos: for the day cometh wherein thy sons shall eat of the fruit of the fig: yea, the vine shall yield new grapes; and the fig-tree shall be no more barren.

"For the interpretation of hidden things is at hand; and men shall eat of the precious fruits of God.

"They shall eat manna from heaven; and shall drink of the river of Salem.

"The Lord maketh all things new: He taketh away the letter to establish the spirit.

"Then spakest thou with veiled face, in parable and dark saying: for the time of figs was not yet."

The Unfolding of Spiritual Sense It was then the development of the woman in Hezekiah's consciousness, the unfolding of his spiritual sense, the deep-

*"Clothed with the Sun," by Anna Kingsford. M. D., pp. 252, 253.

ening of his appreciation of the love of God, together with the overcoming of sin that healed him: it was not literally a poultice of figs.

When the fig tree bears fruit in our consciousness, then it is that we gain dominion over sickness and disease.

The Leaf for Medicine The materialist may further assert that Ezekiel tells us plainly that while the fruit of the *trees planted by the river is to be for meat, the leaf is to be for medicine. These trees of Ezekiel's vision are the trees of life mentioned in the 22nd chaptr of Revelation:

> †"In the midst of the street of it, and on either side of the river, was there the tree of life, which bare twelve manner of fruits, and yielded her fruit every month: and the leaves of the tree were for the healing of the nations."

The Tree of Life This tree of life (or good) stands as the direct opposite of the tree of knowledge of good and evil, or the belief in a power opposed to omnipotent Good. It is only when we believe and indeed know that Good is omnipotent that we are truly healed of our diseases.

Spiritual Inhalations The botanist tells us that a tree breathes through its leaves. God is the Breath of Life: as He exhales, the universe comes into being. Man should inhale spiritually all beauty and goodness, for such spiritual inhalations are life and health to him: they are the leaves for the healing of the nations.

*Ezekiel, xlvii:12.
†Revelation, xxii:2.

Each good thought, each loving action, is a spiritual breath, a leaf plucked from the tree of life.

The Vain Search for Healing   Thousands of suffering mortals, weary and sin-sick, search in vain for healing by the use of material means. When will they learn to "go up into Gilead, and take balm?"

The following from the book of Jeremiah bears on this subject:

> *"For thus saith the Lord, Thy bruise is incurable, and thy wound is grievous.
>
> "There is none to plead thy cause, that thou mayest be bound up: thou hast no healing medicine."

Go Up into Gilead   †"Go up into Gilead, and take balm, O virgin, the daughter of Egypt: in vain shalt thou use many medicines; for **thou shalt not be cured.**"

> ‡"Babylon is suddenly fallen and destroyed: howl for her; take balm for her pain, if so be she may be healed.
>
> "We should have healed Babylon, but she is not healed: forsake her, and let us go everyone into his own country."

And again in the New Testament we read that there was

> ‖"a certain woman, which had an issue of blood twelve years,
>
> "And suffered many things of many physi-

*Jeremiah. xxx:12, 13.   ‡Jeremiah. li:8. 9.
†Jeremiah. xlvi:11.   ‖St. Mark. v:25-29, 34.

The Woman who "Suffered" Many Things of Many Physicians" cians, and had spent all that she had, and was nothing bettered, but rather grew worse,

"When she had heard of Jesus, came in the press behind, and touched his garment.

"For she said, If I may touch but his clothes, I shall be whole.

"And straightway the fountain of her blood was dried up; and she felt in her body that she was healed of that plague.

.   .   .   .

"And he said unto her, Daughter, thy faith hath made thee whole; go in peace, and be whole of thy plague."

Solomon encourages us with the declaration:

*"A merry heart doeth good like a medicine."

How Spiritual Healing is Accomplished It is evident then that a man should be merry: that he should express a sense of harmony, peace and joy; but this harmony must be real, and not assumed: it should well up from the pool of Siloam, which is in the centre of the garden of the soul. There is no real peace or true spiritual healing to be found in matter. Spirit is the only power, and divine Mind the only physician. The daughter of Egypt, in other words, the soul enslaved by matter, must go up into Gilead, where the only balm is to be obtained.

The Spiritual Interpretation of Gilead Now Gilead is a †"strong rocky" position in "a mountainous district, east of the Jordan." It will be remembered that it

*Proverbs, xvii:22.
†Analytical Concordance to the Bible, by Robert Young, LL. D., p. 390.

was the east wind that rolled back the Red Sea. In this instance it was an eastern, strong, rocky district where healing was to be found. It is the rock Christ Jesus on which we must build our superstructure of truth and love. Without divine Light which comes from the east, without the presence of Christ the chief corner stone or rock, there can be no spiritual healing.

Material Medicine Removes Effects The critic may observe that Solomon uses the words "like a medicine," and therefore we are to conclude that a medicine will do us good. Material medicine at its best can only remove effects: it does not touch the real cause of the disease. Disease then will never permanently disappear until such time as man realizes that divine Love is ever present and omnipotent. He must not only realize it: he must make it the principle and the guilding star of his everyday life. Materialists may say that this is not practical, but nevertheless every knee must bow to this Truth.

The Epileptic Healed As Christ descended from the mount of transfiguration

*"there came to him a certain man, kneeling down to him, and saying,

"Lord, have mercy on my son: for he is lunatick and sore vexed: for ofttimes he falleth into the fire, and oft into the water."

This man's son was evidently suffering from what would to-day be called epileptic fits, and the interesting thing about this case is that the disciples were unable to heal the sufferer.

*St. Matthew, xvii:14. 15.

Subtle and Deep-Seated Error We are sometimes told that when a person is not healed it is because God is not willing to relieve him of his sufferings. Jesus, however, gave no such answer as this to his disciples: on the contrary he rebuked them sharply, upbraided them for their unbelief and further taught them that this type of error could only be destroyed by prayer and fasting. He fully understood that it was only through communion with God, and abstaining or fasting from everything material, that man could perform miracles or marvelous works, especially when, as in this case, the error was subtle and deep-seated. Christ proved that it was God's will that the boy should be healed by at once casting out the error, for "the child was cured from that very hour."

The True Meaning of Fasting There are many people who believe that fasting consists in abstaining from certain varieties of food; but this kind of abstinence was not what Christ meant by fasting. Fasting must be primarily mental, for no man will ever become spiritual simply through abstaining from meat and other articles of diet. Fasting may exclude the eating of meat, but we should always remember that it is not that which entereth into a man but that which cometh out of him which defileth him. Christ in his teaching made this truth very clear, and there are many passages in the Bible which uphold it.

We obtain the true meaning of fasting from that ancient Scripture the Mahabharata. Nothing could be more beautifully or lucidly expressed than the definition there given of true fasting. Unfortunately the vast majority of the natives of India no more comprehend the deeper or esoteric meaning of their Scriptures than the average Christian understands his Bible. There are many sacred books, all of which contain the Truth, but men have obscured revelation by dogma which is solely the result of ignorance and superstition.

Holiness Essential *"Those high-souled persons that do not commit sins in word, deed, heart, and soul, are said to undergo ascetic austerities, and not they that suffer their bodies to be wasted by fasts and penances. He that hath no feeling of kindness for relatives cannot be freed from sin, even if his body be pure. That hard-heartedness of his is the enemy of his asceticism. Asceticism, again, is not mere abstinence from the pleasures of the world. He that is always pure and decked with virtues, he that practises kindness all his life, is a Muni, even though he may lead a domestic life. Such a man is purged of all his sins. **Fasts and other penances cannot destroy sins, however much they may weaken and dry up the body that is made of flesh and blood. The man whose heart is without holiness, suffers torture only by undergoing penances in ignorance of their meaning.** He is never freed from sin by such acts. The fire he worshippeth doth not consume his sins. It is in consequence of holiness and virtue alone that men attain to regions of blessedness and fasts and vows become efficacious."

As previously stated, it was after Christ's transfiguration, which took place in a high mountain, that

*The Mahabharata, Vol. II, p. 614.

Spiritual Healing Power Brought down from the Mountain he healed the lunatic; and in like manner it was after coming down from the mount where he had delivered the beatitudes that he healed a leper and the centurion's servant.

The reader is again reminded that the high mountain so frequently referred to in Scripture is spiritual exaltation or illumination, and it is after this illumination that one is able to heal sickness in oneself and others. We must bring this spiritual light down from the mountain into the world in order that sin and misery may be dissipated and destroyed.

Absent Treatment The interesting feature in the healing of the centurion's servant is that Christ healed him at a distance. Christ of course knew that it was no more difficult to heal by speaking the word than it was by laying his hands on the sick man; but Christ marvelled at the centurion's faith. The healing of the servant was instantaneous for we read:

*"Jesus said unto the centurion, Go thy way; and as thou hast believed, so be it done unto thee. And his servant was healed in the selfsame hour."

All sense of material loss, and the various limitations of the senses must be put aside if one is to practice spiritual healing.

Spiritual Mysteries The materialist is continually hurling scornful epithets and sarcasm at the spiritual healer, and this scorn is only natural, since spirit-

*St. Matthew, viii:13.

ual mysteries can be discerned through spiritual sense alone. A sharp line of demarcation should be drawn between worldly wisdom and spiritual understanding. It was Christ's understanding, or knowledge of God as omnipotent, omnipresent and omniscient, which enabled him to perform these miracles.

Miracles Are Divinely Natural
The day of miracles has not passed. So long as God is God, just so long will the working of miracles be possible. The sooner the student realizes that miracles are divinely natural the quicker will he be able to follow in Christ's footsteps, and do the works that he did. To maintain that the day of miracles is past is illogical and short-sighted. Every thinking man must realize that what could be accomplished two thousand years ago can be accomplished to-day. And he is wise if he will disabuse his mind of preconceived notions and dogmas, if he will honestly try to comprehend the teachings of Christ, and will then demonstrate their truth by following Christ's command to go into all the world, healing the sick and preaching the gospel. There is surely no other proof that man possesses this spiritual understanding than by his possession of power to preach the gospel in such a manner that the sick and sinful are healed. Theories are but theories, and it is not the dreamer soaring in the coluds and never coming down to earth, but the practical mystic, who makes the world better through his living in it.

Love is Principle
After all, this living for others should be our aim, for it is only the man who loses his life who truly finds it. Love alone is Principle; without Love there can be no true happiness;

and Love means that man should forget self in his desire to lift another's burden. For selfishness is hell, while Love is heaven; and it can be truthfully said that no selfish man is really happy. Love is both the Law and the fulfilling of the Law. The very heart and soul of Christ's teaching is Love. It is a priceless treasure, and the man who is willing to sell all in order to gain it, is wise indeed.

The Mystic Exodus from the Mystic Egypt   The following excerpts from the beautiful ancient hymn—the "Hymn to the Planet-God"—illustrate the importance of interpreting ancient documents allegorically. To interpret this hymn literally would be foolishness in the extreme. It is worthy of careful study, and its spiritual interpretation throws a flood of light on the various statements made throughout this book.

Those of my readers who are unacquainted with the wonderful writings of Anna Kingsford will be interested in the following:

*"The story of the recovery of this hymn is told in 'The Life of Anna Kingsford.' * * * Mr. Maitland * * * says: 'The method (of its recovery) was such as to constitute it a proof positive of the great doctrine set forth in it, the doctrine of Reincarnation; for it was as one of a band of initiates, making solemn procession through the aisles of a vast Egyptian temple, chanting it in chorus, that Mary (Anna Kingsford), being asleep, recollected it.'"

Notice "the mystic Exodus from the mystic Egypt, the Exodus of the soul from the power of the body."

*The Bible's Own Account of Itself, by Edward Maitland, B.A., p. 56.

"HYMN TO THE PANET-GOD"

*"Evoi, Iacchos, Lord of the Sphinx: who linkest
the lowest to the highest; the loins of the wild beast to
the head and breast of the woman.

*   *   *   *   *   *   *   *

"Yea, blessed and holy art thou, O Master of
Earth: Lord of the cross and of the tree of salvation.

"Vine of God, whose blood redeemeth; bread of
heaven, broken on the altar of death.

"There is corn in Egypt; go thou down into her,
O my soul, with joy.

*   *   *   *   *   *   *   *

"But beware lest thou become subject to the flesh,
and a bond-slave in the land of thy sojourn.

"Serve not the idols of Egypt; and let not the senses
be thy taskmasters.

"For they will bow thy neck to their yoke; they will
bitterly oppress the Israel of God.

*   *   *   *   *   *   *   *

"Thy house shall be smitten with grievous plagues;
blood, and pestilence, and great darkness; fire shall
devour thy goods; and thou shalt be a prey to the
locust and creeping thing.

*   *   *   *   *   *   *   *

"Until the body let the soul go free; that she may
serve the Lord God.

"Arise in the night, O soul, and fly, lest thou be
consumed in Egypt.

*   *   *   *   *   *   *   *

*The Bible's Own Account of Itself, by Edward Maitland B. A., pp. 59-61.

"Let the rod of thy desire be in thy right hand; put the sandals of Hermes on thy feet; and gird thy loins with strength.

"Then shalt thou pass through the waters of cleansing, which is the first death in the body.

"The waters shall be a wall unto thee on thy right hand and on thy left.

* * * * * * * *

"All the horsemen of Egypt and the chariots thereof; her princes, her counsellors, and her mighty men:

"These shall pursue thee, O soul, that fliest; and shall seek to bring thee back into bondage.

* * * * * * * *

"Thou shalt wash thy robes in the sea of regeneration; the blood of atonement shall redeem thee to God.

* * * * * * * *

"Who hath redeemed thee from the dominion of the body, and hath called thee from the grave, and from the house of bondage,

"Unto the way of the Cross, and to the path in the midst of the wilderness;

* * * * * * * *

"But be thou of good courage, and fail thou not; then shall thy raiment endure, and thy sandals shall not wax old upon thee.

"**And thy desire shall heal thy diseases**; it shall bring streams for thee out of the stony rock; it shall lead thee to Paradise."

* * * * * * * *

CPSIA information can be obtained
at www.ICGtesting.com
Printed in the USA
BVHW02s1638020218
506830BV00004B/258/P